Gratitude For Happiness

How to Exercise your Gratitude Muscles

Ged Cusack

First published in the US in 2017

Copyright © Ged Cusack, 2017

The moral right of the author has been asserted.

All rights reserved.

No part of this publication may be reproduced, stored in a retrieval system, or transmitted, in any form or by any means, without the prior permission in writing of the author, nor be otherwise circulated in any form of binding or cover other than that in which it is published and without a similar condition including this condition being imposed on the subsequent purchaser.

ISBN 978-0-473-47721-9

Cover design by Carlos Lacson

DISCLAIMER

This publication is designed to provide competent and reliable information regarding the subject matter covered. However, it is sold with the understanding that the author and the publisher are not engaged in rendering legal, financial or other professional advice. Laws and practices often vary from state to state and country to country and if legal or expert assistance is required, the services of a professional should be sought. The author and publisher specifically disclaim any liability that is incurred from the use or application of the contents of this book.

The publisher does not have any control over and does not assume any responsibility for authors of third party websites and their content.

CONTENTS

Introduction 1
How to Use This Book 6
Chapter One   Finances 9
    1.   Wages & Income 10
    2.   Assets & Cashflow 11
    3.   Credit 13
    4.   Mortgage 15
    5.   Pensions 16
    6.   Miscellaneous Finances 17
Chapter Two   Health & Body 21
    1.   Senses 22
    2.   Nutrition 28
    3.   Exercising 30
    4.   Mental Health 32
    5.   Injuries 34
    6.   Illness & Disease 36
    7.   General Attributes & Qualities 38
    8.   Accidents 41
Chapter Three   Circumstances & Surroundings 45
    1.   Basic Living Circumstances 45
    2.   Beautiful Views 47
    3.   Climate 49
    4.   Air 50
    5.   Fire 51

6.	Water	53
7.	Celestial Entities	54

Chapter Four   Relationships 57

1.	Love	57
2.	Close Friends	59
3.	Breakups	61
4.	Other People's Relationships	63
5.	Families	65
6.	Distance	67
7.	Gifts	68
8.	Life & Death	70
9.	Casual Acquaintances	72

Chapter Five   Material Possessions & Services 75

1.	Physical Necessities	76
2.	Physical Luxuries	78
3.	Physical Luxuries continued	80
4.	Available Services	82
5.	Available Services continued	83

Chapter Six   Careers & Skills 86

1.	Careers	86
2.	Education	88
3.	Progress	90
4.	Creativity	92
5.	Self Confidence	94
6.	Personal Development	96

7.	General Skills	98
8.	Our Own Success	101
9.	The Success of Others	102

Chapter Seven   Time 106

1.	Prioritization	107
2.	Perception	109
3.	Delays	111

Chapter Eight   Passions & Contributions 114

1.	Passion	114
2.	Sports & Pastimes	116
3.	Hobbies	118
4.	Contribution	119

Chapter Nine   Travel 124

1.	Overcoming Travel Adversity	124
2.	Little Things Making a Difference	126
3.	Travelling with Empathy for Others	128
4.	Shorter Journeys	130
5.	Exotic Experiences	131

APPENDIX 134

A.1	Alternative ways to use this book	135
A.2	Reducing your list to three statements	139
A.3	Suggestions on documenting your statements	141
A.4	Your consolidated statements	144
A.5	Glossary	164
A.6	About the author	173

This book is dedicated to my amazing family.

My elderly mother who turned eighty-eight this year is a beacon of energy who never ceases to amaze me.

My brother Peter and my sisters Trish and Teresa have always supported me throughout my life.

My son Lee is an inspiration, growing into an amazing human being with very little input from me.

I credit my family with always providing me the space to be who I am and allowing me to thrive.

Extra thanks go out to my amazing friend and editor Jennifer Manson.

HOW TO EXERCISE YOUR GRATITUDE MUSCLES

Introduction

This Book Is Written To Benefit You

By focusing on the things that you can be grateful for as opposed to a sense of lack it will help attract more things that you can be grateful for and increase your happiness.

Your Gratitude muscles are like any other muscles in that if you haven't used them for a while they may have become weak. They will become stronger the more you use them and the purpose of this book is to provide you the tools to do that.

> *"Feeling gratitude and not expressing it is like wrapping a present and not giving it"* – **William Arthur Ward**

In every one of the courses and books that I have invested in for my own self-discovery, I have always found at least one useful thing to take away.

Perhaps it is because I approach learning with anticipation and because I am actively looking, that I always seem to find something useful. Even the smallest kernel can grow and provide an enormous return on investment.

My wish for everyone reading this book is that you find plenty of useful nuggets that will enhance your life.

Please look through these chapters with an anticipation that you will find the gems that you seek; this will help you find them.

GRATITUDE FOR HAPPINESS

"Enjoy the little things, for one day you may look back and realize they were the big things" – **Robert Brault**

For years I have heard about the power of gratitude and how the truly rich and successful use gratitude as the secret sauce for their happiness. I personally deem that by finding things to be grateful for it has helped me maintain a positive attitude throughout some pretty gruesome times in my life.

The things that you are grateful for should never be considered too small or trivial. If you begin to express gratitude for the small things, you are exercising your gratitude muscles and this will help you find bigger things to be grateful for later.

This is not a competition where you are searching for others less fortunate in order to feel better about yourself. In order to benefit from the act of gratitude you must show appreciation for what you have.

By all means observe others but purely for contrast so that you can reaffirm what you do have. Your prime goal is always to focus on your merits and be grateful for them.

Why This Book Is Laid Out This Way

In order to grow your gratitude muscles you need to exercise them so this book is designed to provide as much support and resources as possible to facilitate those workouts. By providing you multiple exercises you are challenged to work through this book actively rather than just reading a book and taking no action.

In the past, whenever someone presented me with a blank piece of paper and asked me to make a list of goals, dreams or things to be grateful for, I literally drew a blank. Some may find it easier than others to work with a blank sheet but I'm going to assume that you picked up this book because you're willing to accept assistance.

In order to expedite your gratitude journey I have provided you with over four hundred and ninety sample statements that you can use to kick start your own lists of statements. These statements cover a broad spectrum of subjects in order to ensure that there is something of relevance for you. A large percentage of these statements are my personal statements that I have used to build my own happiness.

I have divided the statements up into individual subjects within each chapter and the statements encompass varying degrees of gratitude, to allow you to start being grateful at any level.

The statements provided in this book can be used as they are or can be adapted to specifics more relevant to you; their main purpose is to help you focus on gratitude rather than lack.

You may decide to adapt one of the sample statements for use in a different chapter and that is your choice. This book and all of the information inside is provided solely for you to use in any way that best helps with your gratitude.

For the samples in this book I have chosen to start all of my statements with the same words "*I am happy and grateful that…*" This repetition is to make it easy for you to remember. The use of the word "happy" in the statements is to reinforce the fact that you are using gratitude to build your happiness. If you prefer to start with "Today I am grateful…" or any other phrase, feel free to keep it simple or get creative with whatever resonates best for you.

Most of the sample statements include the benefits for the subject of that statement. I encourage you to initially include these benefits for your own gratitude statements to fortify their power. When you start condensing your statements down later you can dispense with stating the benefits.

At the end of each section of statements I have provided an exercise and the space for you to complete your own gratitude statement. I have already started your statements with that phrase "_I am happy and grateful that_".

I encourage you to write on the pages but if it makes you feel more comfortable use a pencil.

I know how frustrating it can be to have to carry extra notebooks around so I have attempted to allow you to keep the exercises and information all in one place.

Perceptions of Your Status
We all hail from different backgrounds and beginnings and there is no such thing as a perfect person by every standard.

If we only compare ourselves to others we may find that we fall short but the reason we feel superior or inferior to others is largely dependent on our own perception.

The term "Keeping up with the Joneses" is based on the premise that others have more than us and that we are always striving to have as much as them. This is a first world problem as the truly poor are more concerned with basics such as food and shelter, rather than having the latest smartphone or new toy.

My intention in this book is not to equate your status with the status of any other reader or even mine. I am eternally grateful for the benefits that I have been given (and continue to experience) in my life however they are perceived by others. We live in an age where we have more opportunities than at any other time in our history but you need to be open to those opportunities. If you focus on what you are grateful for it will attract more positive opportunities and make your life happier.

Failures & Learnings

So many of the world's successful people recognize that failures can be beneficial on the journey to success. By learning from our failures we can turn them into successes.

Most of us have heard that it took Thomas Edison thousands of attempts to achieve a working light but when we flick a switch to light up our residence we don't focus on all the times that he failed, but on the fact that we now have electric lighting.

> "I have not failed, I have just found 10,000 ways that don't work" – **Thomas A. Edison**

Whenever you are focusing on the lack of something I encourage you to treat that as a learning. Use the feeling of lack purely as a contrast to allow you to focus on how you can be grateful about that situation.

Let's assume that you drop a dozen eggs and six of them break. You could either decide to focus on the fact that you have lost six eggs or be grateful that you still have six eggs left.

It's your choice where you direct your focus.

I encourage you to make gratitude a part of your life from this day forward and I congratulate you for making a start by purchasing this book.

Buying a book and taking no action will not produce any results so come with me to the next section and learn how to use this book to maximize your results.

How to Use This Book

My ultimate goal for this book is for you to develop an ongoing habit of gratitude that will enhance your happiness. There are varied opinions in how long it takes to create a habit (ranging from twenty-one to sixty-six days) but for this book we are going to stick with the twenty-one day period.

The main objective is for you to develop a minimum of three personal gratitude statements as a tool to reinforce your gratitude.

Those three statements will then be used for a twenty-one day period to develop your habit.

I have broken down the process into two easy stages:

Stage One
- Commit to following this process for the next twenty-one days
- Read the book at your own pace during this twenty-one day period using the exercises at the end of each section to reinforce your gratitude.

HOW TO EXERCISE YOUR GRATITUDE MUSCLES

- For each of these twenty-one days start your morning by writing five statements of the things that you are grateful for.
- Before retiring for bed each night read your five statements from that morning.
- At the end of the twenty-one days you should have approximately one hundred and five statements to choose from. If you have less because you duplicated some statements don't feel bad. The process is designed to start exercising your gratitude muscles and not to add to your stress.
- Choose the top three statements from your collection that you resonate most with or that you find most empowering and note those down.

Stage Two
- Commit to following this process for the next twenty-one days
- Ensure that you keep your top three statements close at hand.
- For each of these twenty-one days read your three statements first thing in the morning and last thing at night (preferably out loud).
- Also read your three statements at least once more on each of the twenty-one days at a time that suits you.

By completing this process you should now have a solid foundation of gratitude and have noticed that your happiness levels have increase exponentially.

"The journey of a thousand miles begins with one step" – **Lao Tzu**

Alternative Ways to Use This Book

The instructions on how to use this book have been condensed to allow you to dive into the process and start reaping the benefits. If you want suggestions on alternative ways to use this book, including how to narrow down your lists to the top three statements, how to document your top three statements or alternative processes to reach your top three statements faster, see the appendices at the back of this book.

Chapter One   Finances

One of the most emotionally charged subjects affecting our lives is our views of finance. If you feel that you are experiencing a lack of financial success it can create overwhelming feelings of both inadequacy and failure.

If your first thought when you view an advertisement for a holiday destination or a luxury item is *"I can't afford that"* then you need to readjust your thinking.

One of our main struggles is that we tend not to realize how fortunate we really are. By paying attention to what we actually have (as opposed to what we don't have) and learning to gratefully appreciate that, we take the first steps to addressing our issues.

> *"Gratitude is a currency that we can mint for ourselves and spend without fear of bankruptcy"* – **Fred De Witt Van Amburgh**

One suggested exercise for financial gratitude is carrying $100 (or a similar amount) in the back of your wallet but never spending it. The concept here is that when you are in a store you are grateful that you can afford to make a purchase but you choose not to. Unfortunately not everyone has a spare $100 so I prefer to just repeat the statement *"That purchase is not currently a priority for me"*. By switching your mindset from a sense of lack to a situation of prioritizing you do not need any excess funds to enact this.

Throughout this chapter we are going to look at various areas of finance and statements that you can use to exercise your gratitude muscles in this area.

1. Wages & Income

If you are working for a wage there is every likelihood that you believe that your wages aren't high enough. Most of the time the reason that we aren't happy with our wages is that we have set our value too low. There's an old quote by Jessie B. Rittenhouse (below) that I have used over the years as a reminder that my only limitations are the limits I set on myself.

> "I bargained with Life for a penny, and Life would pay no more, However I begged at evening When I counted my scanty store; For Life is just an employer, he gives you what you ask, but once you have set the wages, Why, you must bear the task. I worked for a menial's hire, only to learn, dismayed, that any wage I had asked of Life, Life would have paid" – **Jessie B. Rittenhouse**

Whatever kind of promotion ladder or pay structure you are on there may be ways and means to make more money; but you must practice gratitude for what you already have.

I have no doubt that there are people around the world who are not as fortunate as you, so instead of worrying about what you don't have, rejoice for what for you do have.

Below is a list of the statements that I use to reaffirm what I have to be grateful for in this area:

HOW TO EXERCISE YOUR GRATITUDE MUSCLES

- I am happy and grateful that I receive an ongoing monthly wage that allows me to cover my purchases.
- I am happy and grateful that I have the freedom to determine how I earn my living and this freedom adds to my happiness.
- I am happy and grateful that there are cheap and nutritious foods such as oats available to me so that I can eat well on my current income.
- I am happy and grateful that I open the mailbox and there are monthly book royalty checks inside.
- I am happy and grateful that I built a part time business and I can benefit from the extra income and the tax benefits.
- I am happy and grateful that I built an online business so that I can earn income from anywhere that I have access to my laptop.
- I am happy and grateful that by being self-employed I can choose to set my wages.

Exercise 01   Wages & Income

I invite you now to complete at least one personal statement in this area that resonates with you. You can utilize part or all of any of the statements above or use something more personal to yourself.

*I am happy and grateful that*_____

_____

2. Assets & Cashflow

I find it interesting that some of us don't have enough assets or cashflow and some of us don't realize how fortunate we are.

GRATITUDE FOR HAPPINESS

If you suddenly received one million dollars today would you still go to work tomorrow? I have asked that question of friends who were mortgage free and had reasonable savings (yet were earning less than $100,000 a year) and they said it wasn't enough. When I raised the number to ten million they said they still weren't sure if that was enough. We tend to overestimate what we need and underestimate what we have so I want you to focus on what you have.

"Price is what you pay. Value is what you get" – **Warren Buffett.**

Below is a list of the statements that I use to reaffirm what I have to be grateful for in this area:

- I am happy and grateful that I have enough cashflow to allow me to be financially comfortable.
- I am happy and grateful that I have choices on how to use my assets to maximize their benefits.
- I am happy and grateful that I receive royalty payments from my book sales as these payments contribute towards my expenses.
- I am happy and grateful that I am attracting money to me as it helps me vibrate at a positive level.
- I am happy and grateful that I can afford to visit the doctor and be proactive as a check-up can pre-empt any illnesses before they become an issue.
- I am happy and grateful that there are cheap activities such as dancing available to me as this means that I can enjoy company on a low budget.

HOW TO EXERCISE YOUR GRATITUDE MUSCLES

Exercise 02   Assets & Cashflow

I invite you now to complete at least one personal statement in this area that resonates with you. You can utilize part or all of any of the statements above or use something more personal to yourself.

*I am happy and grateful that*_____

_____

3. Credit

Despite some of the historical sayings about credit such as "Never a borrower or a lender be", there are some benefits to credit if it is used correctly. You can try to ignore credit card debt and choose to focus on other areas of your financial state but we have all experienced the issue that when we try not to think about something it is all we can think about. If you have to focus on your credit card I suggest that you think of the benefits.

On more than one occasion I have had a credit card bill showing that I owed over ten thousand dollars so I understand that when you have that sickening feeling in your stomach it can make it hard to focus on gratitude.

"Gratitude is riches, complaint is poverty" – **Doris Day**

When you are vibrating at a low level and feeling lack it is especially important to focus on your gratitude to raise your vibrations.

GRATITUDE FOR HAPPINESS

Below is a list of the statements that I use to reaffirm what I have to be grateful for in this area:

- I am happy and grateful that my credit rating allowed me to secure credit lending.
- I am happy and grateful that I am able to service my credit card balance.
- I am happy and grateful that my credit card allows me a thirty day interest free loan as I pay off the full balance at the end of each month.
- I am happy and grateful that my credit card allows me to make purchases online and provides added protection for those purchases.
- I am happy and grateful that my credit card allows me to make secure purchases whilst travelling overseas.
- I am happy and grateful that I am allowed to purchase household goods on hire purchase as this credit has allowed me essentials such as a refrigerator throughout my life.

Exercise 03   Credit

I invite you now to complete at least one personal statement in this area that resonates with you. You can utilize part or all of any of the statements above or use something more personal to yourself.

*I am happy and grateful that*_____

_____

HOW TO EXERCISE YOUR GRATITUDE MUSCLES

4. Mortgage

A house purchase can be one of the biggest financial outlays in our life and most of us fund that purchase with a mortgage. It can be quite disconcerting that the bank initially owns a lot more of your house than you do and the initial payments are predominantly just paying off the interest on the money that you borrowed.

Rather than focus on your lack of ownership I encourage you focus on the benefits that securing your mortgage has provided you.

Below is a list of the statements that I use to reaffirm what I have to be grateful for in this area:

- I am happy and grateful that I can afford a roof over my own head to protect me from the elements.
- I am happy and grateful that I had enough savings to put a deposit on my house purchase.
- I am happy and grateful that I have been able to amass some equity in my house as it allows me leverage for further borrowing.
- I am happy and grateful that I was able to secure enough funding from my mortgage to cover the purchase price of my house.
- I am happy and grateful that I can afford to provide a house and shelter for my family as this adds to my peace of mind.
- I am happy and grateful that I have only five years left to pay off my mortgage as then I will be mortgage free.

Exercise 04   Mortgage

I invite you now to complete at least one personal statement in this area that resonates with you. You can utilize part or all of any

of the statements above or use something more personal to yourself.

*I am happy and grateful that*_____

_____

5. Pensions

When Colonel Harland David Sanders (of KFC fame) received his first pension cheque he decided that he was worth more than that one hundred and five dollars per month. He used this as motivation to build his fried chicken empire, but at the time that money was all he had to survive on.

There will be people reading this book who are also receiving (or are due to receive) some kind of compensation or pension. Those people may believe that what they are receiving isn't sufficient for their needs.

However big or small your pension is you should be grateful that you are actually receiving it. You can look at ways to supplement pensions but ensure that you focus your gratitude on what you already have.

Below is a list of the statements that I use to reaffirm what I have to be grateful for in this area:

- I am happy and grateful that I invested a small amount in my future in the early years of my career as it has benefitted from compound interest and provided for my retirement.
- I am happy and grateful that my pension supplements my income and allows me to fund some extra luxuries in life.
- I am happy and grateful that my pension supplements my income and allows me to fund the necessities in life.

- I am happy and grateful that my employer provides a great pension plan that provides for my future without me adding further funds to this plan.
- I am happy and grateful that the government provides tax breaks for my investment in my future pension as this makes this an affordable option for me.
- I am happy and grateful that I survived for twenty-two years in the military and it has provided me a free monthly pension for life.

Exercise 05   Pensions

I invite you now to complete at least one personal statement in this area that resonates with you. You can utilize part or all of any of the statements above or use something more personal to yourself.

*I am happy and grateful that*_____

_____

6. Miscellaneous Finances

The issue of finances can encompass so much of our lives that the sections above may not provide enough statements to cover every area.

In order to provide you the maximum potential resources I have added this extra section as a repository for other statements that can enhance your gratitude muscles in the financial area.

"I have a fantastic relationship with money. I use it to buy my freedom" – **Gianni Versace**

GRATITUDE FOR HAPPINESS

As this is a miscellaneous section feel free to let your imagination run wild. If there are any areas of finances that are not covered in the sections above but you feel grateful for then write as many statements as you like.

Below is a list of the statements that I use to reaffirm what I have to be grateful for in this area:

- I am happy and grateful that due to a beneficial exchange rate I received an unexpected $500 when I exchanged £2000 sterling today as bonus cash is always welcome.
- I am happy and grateful that I found a ten dollar bill in my suit pocket from the last time I wore it as when any unforeseen cash flows to me it is always welcome in my life.
- I am happy and grateful that I understand money enough to calculate the change that I am due when I make a cash purchase.
- I am happy and grateful that the low cost of baking goods allows me to make cakes and treats for special occasions.
- I am happy and grateful that there are books on finance available at the library so that I can afford to educate myself for free.
- I am happy and grateful that I live in a country where the health services are affordable so that I can get treatment if I need it.
- I am happy and grateful that I can catch enough fish in the sea to be able to feed my family.
- I am happy and grateful that it costs me nothing financially to determine how I am going to feel on a daily basis.

Exercise 06   Miscellaneous Finances

I invite you now to complete at least one personal statement in this area that resonates with you. You can utilize part or all of any of the statements above or use something more personal to yourself.

*I am happy and grateful that*_____
_____

GRATITUDE FOR HAPPINESS

Chapter Two   Health & Body

At different stages of our life we will all experience different levels of health and wellness. We must accept that although we may be stronger and fitter at different ages, there will always be individuals who are born with greater or lesser abilities than us.

When we consider individuals such as the international speaker and motivator Nick Vujicic (born with no arms and legs) or international theoretical physicist Stephen Hawking (paralysed by ALS for decades) we can see that our perception of health is relative.

> *"For every disability you have, you are blessed with more than enough abilities to overcome your challenges"* — **Nick Vujicic**

> *"My advice to other disabled people would be, concentrate on things your disability doesn't prevent you doing well, and don't regret the things it interferes with. Don't be disabled in spirit as well as physically"* — **Stephen Hawking**

The fact that you are healthy enough to be even reading this book means that you have a lot to be grateful for. I truly believe that the more you focus on the aspects of your own health that you are grateful for the more you will find.

1. Senses

It is a fact that we do not all have the benefits of fully experiencing our senses. Even if you are born with all of your senses, as you progress through your life you are destined for your senses to diminish. Although modern medicine is amazing we still have to accept that we will have shortfalls. Rather than focus on them we should look at what we do have.

Studies show that a lack in one area of our senses can heighten another area of our senses (e.g. blind people tend to develop heightened hearing).

The purpose of this section is to highlight the areas of our senses that we can be grateful for and I encourage you to focus on the parts relevant to you.

a) Hearing

When I began my service in the military we had little in the way of hearing protection. We used to fire large weapons with only small rubber ear plugs to shield our ears. The results of limited hearing protection meant that most of my comrades serving during the same period sustained some hearing loss.

When I completed my military service I expected to receive the same financial compensation that my colleagues had received for the loss of hearing. I had all of the audio tests and voila there was nothing wrong with my hearing at all.

I might sound crazy but at that time I felt a little short changed for not receiving the same financial compensation that my comrades had. I realize that for most of us there is no amount of money that we would accept to voluntarily lose all or part of a sense but I was at the time coming from a poverty mentality.

I recount this episode to show that at times my focus has not been in the correct areas and to reinforce that we should always focus on our strengths. Whatever level of hearing you maintain focus on the positives.

When we hear deaf singers such as Mandy Harvey we realize that concentrating on our strengths and being grateful for them can inspire us to overcome the hands that we are dealt.

Below is a list of the statements that I use to reaffirm what I have to be grateful for in this area:

- I am happy and grateful that I can listen to conversations as it helps me communicate.
- I am happy and grateful that I can hear beautiful music as it feeds my spirit.
- I am happy and grateful that my great hearing allows me to traverse dark places.
- I am happy and grateful that I can listen to the dawn chorus of birds outside my window as they act as a natural alarm clock.
- I am happy and grateful that I can listen to audio books as it allows me to learn whilst driving.
- I am happy and grateful that I can listen to the commentary of a sports game so that even when I can't attend I can follow the game on TV or Radio.

GRATITUDE FOR HAPPINESS

Exercise 07　　　　　Hearing

I invite you now to complete at least one personal statement in this area that resonates with you. You can utilize part or all of any of the statements above or use something more personal to yourself.

*I am happy and grateful that*_____

_____

b) Sight

For those of you with 20/20 vision you may take sight for granted but even if you are someone with visual impairment it doesn't mean that there is nothing to be grateful for.

Since I was a small child I have needed spectacles for reading and as well as the inconvenience and expense of trying to keep up with fashion, like lots of people I had to put up with insults such as "four eyes" at school. Although we may envy perfect sight and feel that needing glasses makes us a lesser person, we should be grateful for even the limited amounts of eyesight that we experience.

I take inspiration from historical figures such as Helen Keller who thrived despite her being blind and deaf from the age of two. If they can be happy with less than I have then I have every reason to be grateful for what I have.

> "The only thing worse than being blind is having sight but no vision" — **Helen Keller**

HOW TO EXERCISE YOUR GRATITUDE MUSCLES

Below is a list of the statements that I use to reaffirm what I have to be grateful for in this area:

- I am happy and grateful that my eyes facilitate depth perception as they allow me to cross the road safely.
- I am happy and grateful that I can recognize the faces of my loved ones as it helps me to maintain strong relationships.
- I am happy and grateful that close up vision can be remedied with the aid of spectacles as this allows me to view intricate details and read.
- I am happy and grateful that my eyes are able to work with 3D glasses as it enhances my movie viewing.
- I am happy and grateful that I am able to see amazing views like the snow topped mountains as this helps to ground me.
- I am happy and grateful that I can distinguish colours as this was a factor in my safety during my previous tenure as an electrician.

Exercise 08   Sight

I invite you now to complete at least one personal statement in this area that resonates with you. You can utilize part or all of any of the statements above or use something more personal to yourself.

*I am happy and grateful that*_____

_____

c) Smell & Taste

I count myself as lucky that I have a limited sense of smell. It is inconclusive as to the reasons for my lack of smell but the fact remains that I have limited capacity to smell. A limited sense of smell also means that the edge has been taken off my taste buds so I tend to prefer strong tasting foods.

As I do not benefit from the pleasant aromas of flowers, strong coffee or great foods I could perceive this absence of smell as a lack but I realize that this is offset by the benefits it presents.

I can cut onions for prolonged periods without my eyes watering, If I choose to undertake a diet I am not tempted by the smell of the baking of fresh donuts or cakes (as I walk past a bakery). If I choose to drink a foul smelling smoothie it isn't foul smelling to me.

Without a lack of smell I would not have all of these benefits so I encourage you to focus on the areas of your smell and taste and concentrate on the positives that you experience in this area.

Below is a list of the statements that I use to reaffirm what I have to be grateful for in this area:

- I am happy and grateful that I can drink healthy smoothies however smelly their contents are and benefit from their properties.
- I am happy and grateful that my limited smell allows me to cut onions without my eyes watering, reducing my potential pain.
- I am happy and grateful that I can enjoy the taste of a glass of red wine on a winter's evening as this gives me pleasure.
- I am happy and grateful that in a crowded elevator my perception of the smells is always pleasant.
- I am happy and grateful that I can avoid the temptation of the smell of fresh donuts when I am trying to eat healthy.
- I am happy and grateful that even with a lack of smell I am still able to taste amazing spicy foods and enjoy their benefits.

HOW TO EXERCISE YOUR GRATITUDE MUSCLES

Exercise 09   Smell & Taste

I invite you now to complete at least one personal statement in this area that resonates with you. You can utilize part or all of any of the statements above or use something more personal to yourself.

*I am happy and grateful that*_____

_____

d) Touch

The word "Touch" tends to conjure up an image of someone reaching out a hand to grasp something but we can feel the touch of another human or our environment on all areas of our body.

There are certain perceptions, such as that a heavy handed male may not appreciate the touch of silk sheets, or that touch only relates to direct skin contact but we all have ways in which we can benefit from touch.

Please ensure that you concentrate on the advantages that you receive through touch.

Below is a list of the statements that I use to reaffirm what I have to be grateful for in this area:

- I am happy and grateful that I can feel the touch of a hug from family or friends to make me feel whole.
- I am happy and grateful that I can feel the texture of a clean set of bedding as it makes me feel like a new person.

- I am happy and grateful that I can feel the touch of my partner's hand and experience the joy that it promotes within me.
- I am happy and grateful that I can feel the warmth as I stroke my dog as this helps me recover faster from ailments.
- I am happy and grateful that I can feel my cat's fur and heartbeat as I stroke her as it has a calming effect on me.
- I am happy and grateful that I can feel the heat from a warm fire in winter as it provides me contrast with the cold which helps me appreciate the heat even more.
- I am happy and grateful that I can feel when certain fruits are ripe just by touching them.

Exercise 10   Touch

I invite you now to complete at least one personal statement in this area that resonates with you. You can utilize part or all of any of the statements above or use something more personal to yourself.

*I am happy and grateful that*_____

_____

2. Nutrition

The constantly changing classifications of food and drink make it hard for us to keep up. One day we are told a food is good for us and the next the same food is promoted as bad for us. Limited finances can also play a part in our diet and we tend to get down on ourselves about our decisions.

HOW TO EXERCISE YOUR GRATITUDE MUSCLES

I have known parents who have gone without food to ensure that their children ate and in those cases it wasn't always the best of food.

Growing up in the north of England I remember having salted dripping flat cakes for school lunch (a large flat bread bun the size of a dinner plate smothered in pork fat and salt). This was very cheap and filling but as you can imagine there was a severe lack of nutrition in that food.

Although I encourage you to avoid fad diets or constantly overeating etc. I challenge you to focus on the aspects of nutrition that you can be grateful for.

Below is a list of the statements that I use to reaffirm what I have to be grateful for in this area:

- I am happy and grateful that I have always had enough food to keep me alive.
- I am happy and grateful that I have a source of fresh drinking water readily available as it is essential for life.
- I am happy and grateful that I am able to choose healthier eating options as the foods that we eat have a large impact on our health.
- I am happy and grateful that I can eat nut products without adverse effects as it makes my choices for my daily diet easier.
- I am happy and grateful that there are natural remedies to soothe an acidic stomach so that should I over indulge on certain foods I can remedy this without side effects.
- I am happy and grateful that there is information readily available online to educate me about nutrition as this makes it easier for me to make healthier choices.

Exercise 11   Nutrition

I invite you now to complete at least one personal statement in this area that resonates with you. You can utilize part or all of any of the statements above or use something more personal to yourself.

*I am happy and grateful that*_____

_____

3. Exercising

Although there may be various theories as to which exercises provide the most benefits, it is hard to dispute that combining some exercise with a balanced diet and sufficient sleep helps to contribute to our health. Our abilities for physical exercise can be limited by our circumstances but they can be further limited by our own perception.

Over the years I have personally sustained injuries to my back and knees which mean that I prefer not to run or cycle long distances. Rather than focus on what I can't do I like to focus on the abilities I have available to me. A brisk walk can provide the benefits of a run without the added stress on the knees and a daily calisthenics workout at home can save time intensive trips to gymnasiums or sports centres.

We are all presented with possibilities to exercise and if we choose to be grateful for those opportunities it will enhance our happiness.

Below is a list of the statements that I use to reaffirm what I have to be grateful for in this area:

HOW TO EXERCISE YOUR GRATITUDE MUSCLES

- I am happy and grateful that I am physically able to exercise as it enhances my quality of life.
- I am happy and grateful that my local council provides some great gym facilities that have allowed me to work out when my funds were low.
- I am happy and grateful that I have enough room in my lounge to carry out a workout routine at any time of the day as this helps me maintain the motivation to exercise daily.
- I am happy and grateful that I get to mow my lawns today as this allows me to make my lawns look better and doubles up as exercise.
- I am happy and grateful that I have the motivation to exercise as soon as I get out of bed in the morning as once it's out of the way I experience the physical benefits for the rest of the day.
- I am happy and grateful that I have learned Wing Chun as it helps with my fitness and also helps to centre me.
- I am happy and grateful that I discovered Laughter Yoga as it helped me get through some challenging times and also gave my abdominal muscles a great workout.
- I am happy and grateful that I have the energy to swing a wood splitter as it allows me to split wood for the fire without the need for a power supply and doubles as a great manual exercise.
- I am happy and grateful that I have broad shoulders as they have allowed me to carry weights throughout the years.
- I am happy and grateful that I had a career in the army as it taught me the importance of exercise.
- I am happy and grateful that I had a good night's sleep as it left me feeling alert and refreshed.

Exercise 12   Exercising

I invite you now to complete at least one personal statement in this area that resonates with you. You can utilize part or all of any of the statements above or use something more personal to yourself.

*I am happy and grateful that*_____

_____

4. Mental Health

The subject of mental health can be a wide ranging subject and the mere words "Mental Health" can make some people feel uncomfortable.

Although this term can refer to counselling, pharmaceutical treatments and other main stream emphasis it can also encompass activities such as meditation, positive thinking and other spiritual aspects that add to our wellbeing.

As a military veteran I noticed an improvement in my own wellbeing after I had completed my service and moved to settle in New Zealand. Our environment can affect our mental wellbeing but so can our activities. I tried out new things such as African drumming and laughter yoga which gained comments from my previous associates that "I had become a hippy".

I am not suggesting that you need to make a drastic change in your life in order to remain mentally healthy. I am merely proposing that by focusing on the positive things in your life you will enhance your mental health.

HOW TO EXERCISE YOUR GRATITUDE MUSCLES

Below is a list of the statements that I use to reaffirm what I have to be grateful for in this area:

- I am happy and grateful that I have experienced the love of animals as this has provided both physical and spiritual comfort when it was needed.
- I am happy and grateful that I can use simple ideas and techniques to help switch my mood quickly and help me feel happy.
- I am happy and grateful that the sound of music helps me relax and calms my brain.
- I am happy and grateful that I awoke alive and well today so that I can continue on my life's journey.
- I am happy and grateful that I can immerse myself in a fiction book as it occupies my mind and provides me healthy escapism.
- I am happy and grateful that I attended African drumming classes as the music and the people I met provided a positive environment that gave me a sense of wellbeing.
- I am happy and grateful that my subconscious mind works tirelessly throughout the night whilst I'm sleeping as this makes me productive without me having to think about it.
- I am happy and grateful that I have the ability to remember times when I was fit and healthy as the mental image helps me get back to that healthy status.
- I am happy and grateful that I have an excellent memory that allows me to retain knowledge as this has served me well and helped me survive precarious situations.
- I am happy and grateful that I feel well in my mental wellbeing as I realize that we are chemical beings and I am fortunate to be chemically balanced.
- I am happy and grateful that my bucket list is always growing as I will always have things to look forward to.

- I am happy and grateful that every experience in life gives me something to be grateful for as a positive outlook enhances my life.
- I am happy and grateful that I am able to plan holidays as they give me hope and something to look forward to.
- I am happy and grateful that I was able to realize that there were things that I couldn't control whilst I was serving in operational theatres (war zones) as by focusing on the positive aspects it enhanced my mental health.
- I am happy and grateful that I can quickly change my outlook for the day by focusing on the positive things in my life. Focusing on the positives quells the negative instincts in my thoughts.

Exercise 13   Mental Health

I invite you now to complete at least one personal statement in this area that resonates with you. You can utilize part or all of any of the statements above or use something more personal to yourself.

*I am happy and grateful that*_____

_____

5. Injuries

As we progress through life we tend to accrue some injuries and it could be argued that the more we exercise the more injuries we accrue. It gives us no benefit to focus on the negative impacts of those injuries.

HOW TO EXERCISE YOUR GRATITUDE MUSCLES

Like many military veterans I accumulated injuries throughout my military career. One of the discs in my spine bulged and my knees took a pounding from the years of abuse. I know of many veterans who lost limbs and even their lives so the fact that I can easily go for a seven or eight kilometre walk on a daily basis means that I feel that I have little to complain about.

Knowing that we are better off than others doesn't always appease our competitive human nature. The fact that a lengthy cycle ride would leave me with considerable aches and pains means that there is the odd moment in my life where I envy people like my friend Chalky who competes for his country in Iron Man Triathlon competitions.

The point is that focusing on what I can't do will not add value to my life, whilst being grateful for what I can do will attract more happiness to me. You don't have to mention the injury in these statements, just physicality areas that you are grateful for.

Below is a list of the statements that I use to reaffirm what I have to be grateful for in this area:

- I am happy and grateful that I am able to walk easily on two legs as it makes my mobility easy.
- I am happy and grateful that I am able to breathe effortlessly as it enhances my quality of life.
- I am happy and grateful that I sometimes have aches in my legs as it reminds me that I have two working legs.
- I am happy and grateful that my bulging discs have recovered somewhat as it has allowed me to maintain practical mobility.
- I am happy and grateful that I can walk briskly unencumbered as it allows me to exercise and maintain a healthy body.

- I am happy and grateful that I survived my military service with all of my limbs intact as there were times that this didn't seem possible.
- I am happy and grateful that I have had corrosive liquid splattered in my eye as washing it out with milk meant that the damage wasn't permanent and I know to wear eye protection in future.
- I am happy and grateful that my body has stood up to the rigours of my past life of abusing it (including drinking excessively) – I was not kind to it early on and this has encouraged me to me more moderate today.

Exercise 14   Injuries

I invite you now to complete at least one personal statement in this area that resonates with you. You can utilize part or all of any of the statements above or use something more personal to yourself.

*I am happy and grateful that*_____

_____

6. Illness & Disease

My focus in this section is not to diminish any major illnesses or diseases that the reader may have experienced. I provide my example here purely as a way of showing that we can find things to be grateful for in areas that you might not imagine.

I am considered by most to be a positive person and I tend to smile a lot but I remember vividly a deployment in Canada where

HOW TO EXERCISE YOUR GRATITUDE MUSCLES

I succumbed to frost nip and this impinged on my smiles. They call it frost nip because it is not as severe as frost bite.

When your ear goes from the consistency of marble to the consistency of rising bread rapidly and feels like someone is hanging off of it (by their teeth) the word nip hardly seems appropriate. The reason I remember it so vividly is that one of my superiors said that this short period whilst my ear was defrosting was the only time I didn't smile in a ten week period.

You may wonder what I could find to be grateful for in this kind of situation. Initially my ear swelled up whenever it was going to snow (a bit like using seaweed for weather forecasting) so that was one bonus. Although I had to keep my ear covered for a few weeks I recovered relatively quickly whereas with frost bite I would have possibly lost my ear.

I encourage you to examine your current situation and look for areas of gratitude that you haven't previously thought of.

Below is a list of the statements that I use to reaffirm what I have to be grateful for in this area:

- I am happy and grateful that I was notified by the doctor that I had raised levels of cholesterol as it allowed me to address the issue early.
- I am happy and grateful that I recover quickly from ailments as it helps me live an active life.
- I am happy and grateful that I am fit and healthy as it enhances my quality of life.
- I am happy and grateful that I have survived frost nip as the memory of the pain I experienced helps me appreciate the feeling of wellness.

- I am happy and grateful that I have a set of healthy lungs as they allow me to breathe.
- I am happy and grateful that I have survived hypothermia and I am alive to recount the occurrence.
- I am happy and grateful that I have a strong immune system that makes me resilient to minor ailments.

Exercise 15   Illness & Disease

I invite you now to complete at least one personal statement in this area that resonates with you. You can utilize part or all of any of the statements above or use something more personal to yourself.

*I am happy and grateful that*_____

_____

7. General Attributes & Qualities

We are born with certain abilities and attributes and these can change as we progress through our lives. Mostly we judge ourselves by other people's standards and by this process we can find perceived issues that detract from our happiness. We should all celebrate our differences and realize that they can be seen as strengths.

As the youngest of four siblings it was a bit perturbing to be the first one to accumulate grey hairs (starting around the age of twenty-five). In our family we are blessed with very healthy hair growth. My father who recently died in his mid-eighties had a full head of hair and a higher dark hair to grey hair ratio than me.

HOW TO EXERCISE YOUR GRATITUDE MUSCLES

My elder brother and I treat the issue of my grey hair as a topic of humour but in a world that seems obsessed by appearance some people can feel disadvantaged by minor physical issues such as this.

Whether you are shorter than the national average height for your gender or slightly above your recommended B.M.I., you should focus on the qualities that you have rather than what others might see as your deficits.

Below is a list of the statements that I use to reaffirm what I have to be grateful for in this area:

- I am happy and grateful that I have ten serviceable toes as they help with me physical balance.
- I am happy and grateful that I have a full head of hair as I personally like the feel of it.
- I am happy and grateful that I have two eyes the same colour as I like the symmetry of that.
- I am happy and grateful that I can touch my toes whilst standing up as it is a metric that helps me measure my fitness.
- I am happy and grateful that I have regular bowel movements as a fully functioning digestive system helps with my overall health.
- I am happy and grateful that I have large energy reserves as they help me to endure time intensive ventures.
- I am happy and grateful that I am generally fit and healthy as this contributes to my quality of life.
- I am happy and grateful that I have a healthy heart as it continues to pumps my life's blood around my body.
- I am happy and grateful that I have a good personal hygiene routine as keeping clean helps maintain my health.

GRATITUDE FOR HAPPINESS

- I am happy and grateful that I can tolerate foods containing gluten without adverse effects as it makes my choices for a daily diet easier.
- I am happy and grateful that I take Echinacea (immune booster) as it helps me to survive time intensive working weekends and long haul flights.
- I am happy and grateful that I have chest hair as it helps to keep me warm in bed on a cold winter's night.
- I am happy and grateful that I have thick skin on the soles of my feet as it insulates me from the cold on a winter's morning.
- I am happy and grateful that I can eat dairy products without adverse effects as it makes my choices for a daily diet easier.
- I am happy and grateful that I still enjoy sexual intercourse as this is a healthy state of affairs.
- I am happy and grateful that I realize that health is wealth as by diverting my focus away from money it adds to my quality of life and money flows to me when my health is addressed.
- I am happy and grateful that my military service conditioned me to survive on small amounts of sleep as it helps me to reach a goal when deadlines are tight.

Exercise 16   General Attributes & Qualities

I invite you now to complete at least one personal statement in this area that resonates with you. You can utilize part or all of any of the statements above or use something more personal to yourself.

*I am happy and grateful that*_____
_____

8. Accidents

However safety conscious we are there are times in our life when we cannot control our environment. The driver on the other side of the road or the pilot of a commercial airplane can make decisions that are outside our control but can have dire consequences for us.

I hope that if you have experienced an accident (or experience one in the future) that the results are positive for you.

I am personally inspired to be grateful in the area of accidents when I consider individuals such as Morris Goodman. Morris survived a serious plane crash in 1981 and although he was given a dire prognosis he beat the odds and recovered largely through his own will power.

> *"You can do, have and be things that people once said that's impossible for you to do and be"* – **Morris Goodman.**

I myself have been a passenger in several vehicles where the person driving collided with another vehicle or object and rather than focus on the crashes I choose to focus on the positive outcomes.

Below is a list of the statements that I use to reaffirm what I have to be grateful for in this area:

- I am happy and grateful that I burnt my finger tip today as it has taught me to be more careful when filling the wood burner in future.
- I am happy and grateful that I have survived several road traffic accidents and am still fit and healthy.

GRATITUDE FOR HAPPINESS

- I am happy and grateful that I have recovered quickly from injuries sustained in accidents as they have taught me to value life.
- I am happy and grateful that I cut the top off of my finger when I was a child as it taught me not to run my finger across cut glass.
- I am happy and grateful that I have seen the results of a blade breaking on an angle grinder as it reminds me to wear a safety visor when grinding.
- I am happy and grateful that I have seen the results of a rifle shot and it ensures that I handle firearms safely.
- I am happy and grateful that I accidentally snapped off the handle of my empty coffee mug whilst I was drying it as this has ensured that I double check my mug handles if they contain hot liquid.

Exercise 17   Accidents

I invite you now to complete at least one personal statement in this area that resonates with you. You can utilize part or all of any of the statements above or use something more personal to yourself.

*I am happy and grateful that*_____

_____

HOW TO EXERCISE YOUR GRATITUDE MUSCLES

GRATITUDE FOR HAPPINESS

HOW TO EXERCISE YOUR GRATITUDE MUSCLES

Chapter Three   Circumstances & Surroundings

Our happiness can be severely impacted by the surroundings and living circumstances that we find ourselves in.

If you use Facebook or YouTube you may have been bombarded by adverts of rags to riches stories and presented with entrepreneurs showing you views of their mansions or tropical islands and other lavish habitat.

I am assuming that most of us are starting from slightly humbler beginnings and although you could focus on the fact that there are better alternatives out there it is more beneficial for you to focus on what you have got.

> *"Not everyone will appreciate the beauty of their surroundings like you do. Spend time with those that do"*
> **– April Mae Monterrosa**

In this chapter we are going to look at your circumstances and surroundings and how you can be grateful for their positive aspects.

1. Basic Living Circumstances

Whether you have a cardboard box or granite block, if you have something to protect you from the elements then you have something to be grateful for. The feelings of inferiority or lack that we impose on ourselves tend to materialise because we are judging ourselves by others' standards.

GRATITUDE FOR HAPPINESS

"There are four types of environments; the one that can help destroy you, the one that can help improve you, the one that can destroy the improved you and the one that can improve the destroyed you. Watch out be vigilant!" – **Israelmore Ayivor**

Whatever your living circumstances there are areas that you can choose to be grateful about but you just need to decide to make that choice.

Below is a list of the statements that I use to reaffirm what I have to be grateful for in this area:

- I am happy and grateful that I have a roof over my head to protect me from the elements.
- I am happy and grateful that I have sports fields across the road from my house so I can watch local sports whenever I want.
- I am happy and grateful that I live in a semi-rural area for the calming peace and quiet outside my bedroom window.
- I am happy and grateful that whilst living in Canada my house had great insulation against the cold temperatures to keep me warm.
- I am happy and grateful that I live so close to an international airport as it reduces my travel time and reduces the stress of worry that I might miss a flight.
- I am happy and grateful that I have a local library that provides close access to the knowledge in books to help me grow. The fact that these facilities are available close & free means there is every reason to utilize them.

HOW TO EXERCISE YOUR GRATITUDE MUSCLES

- I am happy and grateful that I have positive quotes posted around my house as they provide me great inspiration to keep me on a positive track.
- I am happy and grateful that there are trees along the fence in my neighbours' garden as they provide me a free wind break.

Exercise 18   Basic Living Circumstances

I invite you now to complete at least one personal statement in this area that resonates with you. You can utilize part or all of any of the statements above or use something more personal to yourself.

*I am happy and grateful that*_____

_____

2. Beautiful Views

Whether we are standing under a bridge or on a mountain top, the views that we are presented with on a daily basis can move our hearts in various directions. You can choose to be inspired or disheartened by exactly the same views so I implore you to focus on the positive value that you can glean from them.

The views that you observe don't have to be a view from the top of the world or from the bottom of the sea as we can all extract beauty from our everyday environment if we choose to be grateful for the positives.

I think this quote from the great Dale Carnegie sums up this point of different perspectives we can have of the same view.

GRATITUDE FOR HAPPINESS

"Two men looked out from prison bars, one saw the mud, the other saw stars" – **Dale Carnegie**

Below is a list of the statements that I use to reaffirm what I have to be grateful for in this area:

- I am happy and grateful that I can look out of my window at the beautiful flowers in my garden as they are so close yet bring me such joy.
- I am happy and grateful that I can look out of my office window at the park and see all the happy people walking their dogs and spreading their joy to me.
- I am happy and grateful that I have great views of the mountains from my living room as I find these inspiring.
- I am happy and grateful that I live in front of sports fields as I do not have to look onto other houses and the sight of others exercising motivates me to exercise.
- I am happy and grateful that I have looked out over the Canterbury plains from a hot air balloon as it gives me a different viewpoint of the areas surrounding my house.
- I am happy and grateful that modern technology allows me to see the pictures taken from the international space station as they are truly awe inspiring.

Exercise 19   Beautiful Views

I invite you now to complete at least one personal statement in this area that resonates with you. You can utilize part or all of any of the statements above or use something more personal to yourself.

HOW TO EXERCISE YOUR GRATITUDE MUSCLES

*I am happy and grateful that*_____

_____

3. Climate

We all have different views of climates and weather systems. Where some of us view a warm beach holiday as heaven, others see it as hell. Some people see snow as restricting their daily work while others see it as a resource for skiing. I want to challenge you to only focus on the parts of your climate that provide you with positive feelings and joy.

If you enjoy, rain, snow, sun or just a cloudy day then hold those thoughts that promote joy in you. Only you can determine what will make you happy.

Below is a list of the statements that I use to reaffirm what I have to be grateful for in this area:

- I am happy and grateful that I live in a warm, dry place.
- I am happy and grateful that I have free access to a beach.
- I am happy and grateful that I live in a temperate climate because I having experienced people freezing to death in Russia and Canada I know that my circumstances are privileged.
- I am happy and grateful that I get to experience cold mornings as they remind me of the benefits of heating.
- I am happy and grateful that I live in a country that has plentiful rainfall as it enhances all of the colours of the flowers and plants.
- I am happy and grateful that I grew up in a cold place in the north of England so that the early winter mornings of my current habitat seem mild to me.

GRATITUDE FOR HAPPINESS

Exercise 20   Climate

I invite you now to complete at least one personal statement in this area that resonates with you. You can utilize part or all of any of the statements above or use something more personal to yourself.

*I am happy and grateful that*_____

_____

4. Air

The combination of gases that compose the air that we breathe is essential to our existence on the planet.

Most people in the western world take access to fresh air and its benefits for granted but not everyone has that privilege. In this section of the book I want to draw your attention to the advantages that air provides us and I encourage you to focus on those positive aspects.

I have been fortunate to experience the contrast of the negative alternatives to positive air from the smog of Christchurch to polluted air from burning oil fires in Iraq and this contrast has made me appreciate the benefits of clean air even more.

Below is a list of the statements that I use to reaffirm what I have to be grateful for in this area:

- I am happy and grateful that I have fresh air to breathe every day as not only do I love the taste of fresh air but I realize that this privilege is a necessity for me.

HOW TO EXERCISE YOUR GRATITUDE MUSCLES

- I am happy and grateful that the wind helps to dry my clothes on the washing line as this gives them a fresh feel for me.
- I am happy and grateful that my local council enacted clean air initiatives that eliminated the smog from the city air on a winter's morning.
- I am happy and grateful that I can open my windows on a morning to allow fresh air to circulate throughout my house as this provides me a healthier environment.
- I am happy and grateful that my car is designed for lower gas emissions as this helps to protect the environment I live in.
- I am happy and grateful that I experienced the toxic air during the oil fires in Iraq safely as it has enhanced my appreciation for fresh air to breathe.

Exercise 21   Air

I invite you now to complete at least one personal statement in this area that resonates with you. You can utilize part or all of any of the statements above or use something more personal to yourself.

*I am happy and grateful that*_____

_____

5. Fire

Ever since the cave man discovered fire we have used it as a method of heating and cooking. We tend to forget that this basic resource provides us benefits that add to our pleasure and survival.

GRATITUDE FOR HAPPINESS

I am fortunate that in my current rural house I have a wood fire as my primary heating and to supplement my hot water in winter. I could choose to focus on the need to chop and stack wood to feed the fire or to be grateful for all of the benefits that the wood fire provides. I choose to be grateful for the benefits.

Although fire can be destructive and decimate forests and vegetation, combustion animates motors and other useful resources in our environment that provide us with value. Just as in any of the other subjects in this book, you determine where you put your focus. I encourage you to direct your attention to the benefits of fire and the positive emotions it instils within you.

Below is a list of the statements that I use to reaffirm what I have to be grateful for in this area:

- I am happy and grateful that fire provides me the feeling of warmth just by looking at it.
- I am happy and grateful that the fire from my gas stove heats my food and sustains my life.
- I am happy and grateful that commercially manufactured firelighters allow me to start the heating fires in my house easily.
- I am happy and grateful that fire heats my house throughout the winter and provides a cosy feeling for my visitors.
- I am happy and grateful that I can have friends round for a barbeque and cook them a meal on an open fire as it adds flavour to the food and ambiance to the event.
- I am happy and grateful that when the snow cuts off the electricity to my house I still have a wood fire to keep me warm and alive.
- I am happy and grateful that limited crop burning allows new growth of the crops that the farmers supply as my food.

Exercise 22   Fire

I invite you now to complete at least one personal statement in this area that resonates with you. You can utilize part or all of any of the statements above or use something more personal to yourself.

*I am happy and grateful that*_____

_____

6. Water

Our bodies are made up of approximately fifty-five to sixty percent water so it is a fact that we need water for life. With around seventy percent of the earth's surface covered in water it becomes not just a necessity but also provides us resources for so much more than survival. When you take into account the many benefits of water, it provides us a lot to be grateful for.

I have to confess that I am not the best swimmer in the world and my sinuses do not allow me to scuba dive but once I realized that a wet suit could provide me extra buoyancy I took advantage of the options that snorkelling allowed me. I choose to focus on the benefits of a situation and I challenge you to continually do the same.

Whether you are viewing water through the lens of fluids to keep you alive or as a resource in its many forms to be enjoyed, I encourage you be grateful for all of its rewards.

GRATITUDE FOR HAPPINESS

Below is a list of the statements that I use to reaffirm what I have to be grateful for in this area:

- I am happy and grateful that I have fresh clean drinking water readily available as it is essential for life.
- I am happy and grateful that I live in a country that experiences snow as it makes my garden look as tidy as everyone else's in winter.
- I am happy and grateful that I have hot running water readily available so that I can have the joy of a hot shower at any time.
- I am happy and grateful that I have access to rivers and streams as the sound of their flowing waters is very calming.
- I am happy and grateful that the rain feeds the flowers in the gardens and parks that I see on a daily basis as they provide me visual treats that cheer me up.
- I am happy and grateful that the rain contributes to rainbows that add a sense of wonder to my life.

Exercise 23   Water

I invite you now to complete at least one personal statement in this area that resonates with you. You can utilize part or all of any of the statements above or use something more personal to yourself.

*I am happy and grateful that*_____
_____

7. Celestial Entities

The majesty of the stars, the sun, the moon and other celestial entities are all provided for us free by the universe. These resources can give us some of the most amazing visual inspirations.

I have been fortunate to have experienced the dancing northern lights (Aurora Borealis) and some amazing tapestries of stars on the Canadian prairies that have provided me with memories that I will always treasure.

The views that they provide are awe inspiring but we should also take into account their impact on the planet around us.

Wherever you are, as long as you have access to a window (or a door that opens) you should be able to take some comfort and benefit from these amazing creations of nature.

Below is a list of the statements that I use to reaffirm what I have to be grateful for in this area:

- I am happy and grateful that the moon can provide bright light on a dark night to help me walk home safely.
- I am happy and grateful that I have experienced the fantastic light show of the northern lights (Aurora Borealis) as this has provided me amazing memories for life.
- I am happy and grateful that I when I am alone I get to view the stars on a clear night as they make the darkness less lonely.
- I am happy and grateful that the sun enables photosynthesis to grow the plants that feed me.
- I am happy and grateful that the sun can be converted into sustainable energy to power my phones, cars, houses and so much more.
- I am happy and grateful that the sun interacts with the clouds at dusk and dawn to provide me awe inspiring views across the skies.

GRATITUDE FOR HAPPINESS

- I am happy and grateful that the sun's rays warm me on a summer's day as this warmth is both physical and emotional.
- I am happy and grateful that the stars in the night sky show me that there are bigger things in the universe and inspire me on to bigger things.
- I am happy and grateful that the moon stops the earth wobbling on its rotation as this is a service that is seldom recognized but maintains the habitability of our planet.

Exercise 24   Celestial Entities

I invite you now to complete at least one personal statement in this area that resonates with you. You can utilize part or all of any of the statements above or use something more personal to yourself.

*I am happy and grateful that*_____

_____

HOW TO EXERCISE YOUR GRATITUDE MUSCLES

Chapter Four   Relationships

From the moment that we are born to our last breath, our relationships are changing and the quality of these relationships will be determined to some degree by how we view them.

The word relationship tends conjure up thoughts of two people who are linked through marriage or cohabitation but in reality it encompasses all of the interactions throughout our lives.

Because our whole life involves relationships, this provides us so much content to be grateful for. You may believe this area doesn't relate to you because you are an introvert who spends most of your life in front of your computer. I hate to dispel any myths but I feel the need to remind you that you are always in a relationship with yourself and if you are interacting with others online, they are relationships too.

In this chapter I have included sections covering a broad range of the areas of relationships and I encourage you to work through these areas, intensifying your gratitude in these regions.

1. Love

Love is arguably one of the strongest influences on our relationships. Just hearing someone say the words "I love you" can create a warm feeling inside.

During positive times in our lives love comes easily and naturally. When you start a new relationship or you see your new-born child for the first time your love seems to flow effortlessly.

There are also times in our lives when we may feel lonely or depressed and although these are the more difficult times to focus on love, they are the times that we need to the most.

GRATITUDE FOR HAPPINESS

I remember a time shortly after my marriage breakup when my birthday came around. It was the first time in years that I had received no cards or presents. For some unknown reason that year my family overseas hadn't seemed to acknowledge that it was my birthday. There didn't seem a lot of love around at that time and so I determined that I would take control.

I printed off a sheet of A4 paper that said "I LOVE YOU GED" and taped it at the bottom of my bathroom mirror. Each morning when I had a shave I read this statement out aloud and it raised my vibrations 1000%.

By being grateful that I loved myself it allowed me to attract more love into my life.

> *"Do not speak badly of yourself. For the warrior within hears your words and is lessened by them"* – **David Gemmell**

We all have lots of love locked inside us but we don't always know how to unlock it. I challenge to you to focus your love on areas where you can be grateful and use that to raise your vibrations.

Below is a list of the statements that I use to reaffirm what I have to be grateful for in this area:

- I am happy and grateful that I have the unconditional love of my dog as that is always available to me.
- I am happy and grateful that I love myself as I have chosen who I am and I can always be a better person.
- I am happy and grateful that I have learned to love myself as this has provided me the foundation to love another person.

HOW TO EXERCISE YOUR GRATITUDE MUSCLES

- I am happy and grateful that I love life and I feel that each week has the potential to be successful as by setting a positive expectation it attracts positive influences into my life.
- I am happy and grateful that I have learned to accept the love of others as by opening up it has made me a stronger person.
- I am happy and grateful that I saw the first smile from my baby son as this created a love inside me that will last forever.
- I am happy and grateful that I have always had the love of my family as it has provided me with warmth and support for the whole of my life.

Exercise 25   Love

I invite you now to complete at least one personal statement in this area that resonates with you. You can utilize part or all of any of the statements above or use something more personal to yourself.

*I am happy and grateful that*_____

_____

2. Close Friends

Throughout our lives we can build some amazing lasting friendships: best friends whom we may call on as maids of honour or best men and confidants who support us through thick and thin.

You may have mates whom you have known since your early school days or roommates from university and even if you don't have constant contact with these groups or individuals I'm a firm believer that these relationships should be celebrated.

GRATITUDE FOR HAPPINESS

"A friend is someone who gives you total freedom to be yourself"
– Jim Morrison

I am personally fortunate that I served with some amazing people during my military service and this has led to some lifelong friendships that have spanned huge distances and decades of history.

In this section I encourage you to concentrate on the benefits that those relations give you and reaffirm your gratitude for them.

Below is a list of the statements that I use to reaffirm what I have to be grateful for in this area:

- I am happy and grateful that my friends want to visit me as it encourages me to keep my house clean and tidy.
- I am happy and grateful that I have reliable friends who are there for me in times of need as knowing they are there provides me great comfort.
- I am happy and grateful that I have former work colleagues who have developed into lifelong friends.
- I am happy and grateful that I have built lasting friendships over the years as it is a myth that a self-made man grows without the support of others.
- I am happy and grateful that I have friends willing to provide accommodation when I visit their town as it saves me motel bills and provides me an excuse to catch up with them.
- I am happy and grateful that my friends want to contact me as it keeps me on my toes to maintain my relationships.
- I am happy and grateful that I have attracted great mentors into my life as this reinforces the fact that I always get exactly the mentor I need to thrive in any area.

HOW TO EXERCISE YOUR GRATITUDE MUSCLES

- I am happy and grateful that I have a mastermind group of friends who have met for over eight years as they have provided me some very wise counsel over those years.
- I am happy and grateful that I have a good friend who is an editor as she has encouraged and supported me on my writing journey.
- I am happy and grateful that I have diverse in-laws as they all bring different qualities to our relationships.
- I am happy and grateful that my friends' kind words have helped support me when I have needed them.

Exercise 26   Close Friends

I invite you now to complete at least one personal statement in this area that resonates with you. You can utilize part or all of any of the statements above or use something more personal to yourself.

*I am happy and grateful that*_____

_____

3. Breakups

Unless you are extremely fortunate you will have no doubt experienced some kind of relationship breakup in your life. Whether it be the loss of your childhood sweetheart (perhaps the breakup of your parents) or the end of a long term relationship later in your life, we are all touched by this in some way or another.

GRATITUDE FOR HAPPINESS

"Don't put your life on hold so that you can dwell on the unfairness of past hurts"
— **Nick Vujicic**

My three siblings and I have all undergone at least one divorce and have managed to come out of the other side the wiser for them. If we look closely we can find positives from every relationship breakup and although at the time of the breakup our emotions can inhibit positive thoughts, in time we can come to terms with our situation.

"People change and forget to tell each other"
— **Lillian Hellman**

Trying to apportion blame for a breakup is a waste of time, so rather than project on anyone I suggest focusing on the positive learnings from the situation.

Below is a list of the statements that I use to reaffirm what I have to be grateful for in this area:

- I am happy and grateful that I am comfortable in my own company so that I do not need a relationship to validate me.
- I am happy and grateful that the ending of a bad relationship creates space for a better relationship to grow.
- I am happy and grateful that I once attracted a beautiful and intelligent women to marry me.
- I am happy and grateful that I had an amicable divorce so that I didn't lose one of my best friends.

HOW TO EXERCISE YOUR GRATITUDE MUSCLES

- I am happy and grateful that I had a loving relationship that survived for twelve years.
- I am happy and grateful that I have learned and grown as a person from my recent breakup.

Exercise 27   Breakups

I invite you now to complete at least one personal statement in this area that resonates with you. You can utilize part or all of any of the statements above or use something more personal to yourself.

*I am happy and grateful that*_____

_____

4. Other People's Relationships

You can learn from your own relationships but it is sometimes easier for you to be objective when you are looking at other people's relationships.

After the breakup of my own marriage I started to notice that some of my friends were making the same mistakes I had made. They seemed to not realize that they had loving families. They weren't paying attention and weren't being grateful for the things that they had.

Rather than feeling superior or focusing on their mistakes, I used these experiences to provide contrast to what I wanted from my own relationships.

I encourage you to focus on the positive aspects of the relationships of others. You can observe the shortfalls of others but only as a way of identifying the alternatives and to allow you to focus on ways of improving your own relationships.

We can all focus on the positive aspects of others' relationships as a way of attracting it again, rather than as a form of lament.

Below is a list of the statements that I use to reaffirm what I have to be grateful for in this area:

- I am happy and grateful that my parents stayed married for over sixty years as this provides me hope that relationships can last.
- I am happy and grateful that I have experienced my friends treating their partners well and this has helped me to be a better partner in my own relationships.
- I am happy and grateful that I have experienced how my friends interact with their children and this has educated me for my own interactions with children.
- I am happy and grateful that I can celebrate the diversity of my friends' relationships and enrich my own life with the experiences they provide.
- I am happy and grateful that watching my colleagues interact has taught me how to be more flexible in my work relationships.
- I am happy and grateful that I have learned from my friends' mistakes as this has provided me contrast and allowed me to focus on the positive alternatives in my own relationships.

Exercise 28   Other People's Relationships

I invite you now to complete at least one personal statement in this area that resonates with you. You can utilize part or all of any

of the statements above or use something more personal to yourself.

*I am happy and grateful that*_____

_____

5. Families

You may have a positive or a negative relationship with certain members of your family. There are two sayings that spring to mind: "you can choose your friends but you can't choose your family" and "blood is thicker than water".

A certain percentage of people perceive the first statement as a negative because they feel that they are stuck with blood relatives whom they would not choose to associate with otherwise and they perceive the second as a positive because they assume that the bonds of blood ties are strong enough to overcome minor issues.

I appreciate that not all family relationships are perfect and there will be reasons why you may choose to cut ties with family members. Whether it is blood relatives or adopted families, most of us have some positive family experiences.

Growing up as the youngest of four I may seem biased in my Pollyanna view of my childhood; but I also remember less pleasant episodes whilst under the care of my elder siblings. Living near a cemetery and having to use that cemetery as a shortcut to my brother's football games meant that on more than one occasion I was left alone for short periods in a dark cemetery.

Being a little brat I no doubt deserved the odd bout of tough love from my siblings but I also remember one of my sisters singing songs to me at a very early age and the fact that I could always depend on my family's support as a child.

I would like to propose that for the majority of people the benefits of family outweigh the disadvantages. Our early experiences tend to form who we are and if we look closely enough I believe that most of us can find something positive from our family interactions.

Below is a list of the statements that I use to reaffirm what I have to be grateful for in this area:

- I am happy and grateful that my family provide me with constructive criticism as their feedback provides a different perspective that allows me to improve.
- I am happy and grateful that I got to speak to my mother on her eighty eighth birthday as it reminds me how fortunate I am to still have a loving mother.
- I am happy and grateful that I have amazing siblings as they have been incredibly supportive in times of need.
- I am happy and grateful that I have a great bond with my sister as she helps to reinforce my self-confidence.
- I am happy and grateful that events such as marriages and adoption can allow me to grow my family and build strong nurturing relationships with others.
- I am happy and grateful that my siblings are all different as their diversity makes life more interesting.

Exercise 29 Families

I invite you now to complete at least one personal statement in this area that resonates with you. You can utilize part or all of any of the statements above or use something more personal to yourself.

HOW TO EXERCISE YOUR GRATITUDE MUSCLES

*I am happy and grateful that*_____

_____

6. Distance

You have no doubt heard the saying that "distance makes the heart grow fonder" but you may have experienced the alternative emotions of absence and disconnection.

As somebody who was away from my friends and family for many years whilst serving in the military I can relate to that. I currently live in New Zealand and at times miss my siblings in the UK and USA – but as technology has improved life has progressed from the only contact being via snail mail.

Whether we are situated a short drive away or half a world away, the conditions that distance creates can be celebrated or bemoaned. I encourage you to choose to celebrate with gratitude as I do.

Below is a list of the statements that I use to reaffirm what I have to be grateful for in this area:

- I am happy and grateful that modern technology allows me to share life events with relatives and friends around the world.
- I am happy and grateful that when I have been away from friends and relations, the distance has allowed me to examine my relationships and reconnect with added vigour.
- I am happy and grateful that the frequency of international flights allows me to reach friends and family in less than forty eight hours, anywhere on the planet.

- I am happy and grateful that the distance and diverse experiences between my partner and myself provide interesting material for our conversations.
- I am happy and grateful that I have Facebook to remind me of important dates like birthdays as this helps me maintain relationships at a distance.
- I am happy and grateful that most of my friends are a car drive away as it provides anticipation for our meetings that makes the meetings richer.

Exercise 30   Distance

I invite you now to complete at least one personal statement in this area that resonates with you. You can utilize part or all of any of the statements above or use something more personal to yourself.

*I am happy and grateful that*_____

_____

7. Gifts

Whether you are a gift giver or a gift receiver, the act of giving is designed to strengthen relationships.

It might seem obvious that we should be grateful when we receive gifts but if you are familiar with Gary Chapman's book "The Five Love Languages" you will know that we don't all treat gift giving the same. If one partner or friend has a love language of *'gift giving'* and they receive an expression of love from someone whose love language is *'acts of service'* it can mean that they feel short changed as they are expecting a gift and the other wants to perform a service.

Financial circumstances may also have an effect as a gift received might not meet a perceived level.

Although some of us may not understand how anyone can not be grateful for receiving a gift, think of the stereotype of a man buying an unsolicited kitchen utensil for his wife's birthday. I use that example purely as a way of highlighting that good intentions may not elicit the desired response to a gift.

I myself tend to see possessions as just stuff so I actually find it hard to receive gifts and this can be a bit tough on the people around me.

Now that I've showed you some contrast in relation to gift giving, for the rest of this section only focus on the things that you can be grateful for.

Below is a list of the statements that I use to reaffirm what I have to be grateful for in this area:

- I am happy and grateful that I have friends and family who take the time to source gifts for me.
- I am happy and grateful that friends and family choose to spend their hard earned money on me.
- I am happy and grateful that I am valued enough by others to elicit gifts from them.
- I am happy and grateful that I have great neighbours who give me the gift of their time as they cut my lawns whenever I am away travelling.
- I am happy and grateful that I have learned to accept a coffee or a meal from a friend as by allowing them to give and also letting myself receive it benefits us both.

- I am happy and grateful that I can search for just the right gift for friends as the process of research makes me happy.

Exercise 31   Gifts

I invite you now to complete at least one personal statement in this area that resonates with you. You can utilize part or all of any of the statements above or use something more personal to yourself.

*I am happy and grateful that*_____

_____

8. Life & Death

You may be lucky that you have either not experienced death of someone close to you yet or perhaps didn't experience it until later in life. Unfortunately in the modern world we are provided more and more opportunities to experience death close up.

I myself have experienced death in various forms in my life and I know that at the time when you are grieving there seems little to be grateful for.

I have had military friends alive and joking with me and then dead the next day. I've lost a baby shortly before the due date and my father recently passed.

Even though I know I will always miss my father (and I am affected by the other deaths in my life) I choose to focus on life and the positive lessons from death.

Even in times of grief you can focus on the positives in your life and you'll be amazed what you will find.

HOW TO EXERCISE YOUR GRATITUDE MUSCLES

Below is a list of the statements that I use to reaffirm what I have to be grateful for in this area:

- I am happy and grateful that I knew my father for over fifty years as this added wealth of experiences to my life.
- I am happy and grateful that although my father has died he is no longer suffering in pain.
- I am happy and grateful that I was fortunate enough to have the love of my father for over fifty years of my life as that love is priceless.
- I am happy and grateful that during my grief I had the love of a supportive family.
- I am happy and grateful that even though I lost a child I was still able to father another child.
- I am happy and grateful that I have had some great pets throughout my life as they have provided me with unconditional love.
- I am happy and grateful that I have the ability to grieve in my own way as it helps me with closure.
- I am happy and grateful that I got to spend some quality time with my father before he passed as I will cherish those moments forever.
- I am happy and grateful that I had some amazing fun times with my military comrades before they passed.

Exercise 32   Life & Death

I invite you now to complete at least one personal statement in this area that resonates with you. You can utilize part or all of any of the statements above or use something more personal to yourself.

I am happy and grateful that_____

_____

9. Casual Acquaintances

When we refer to relationships we tend to think of our personal long term relationships but forget about our everyday work colleagues and acquaintances. Casual acquaintances and encounters are all relationships of sorts.

One of my favourite exercises in relation to gratitude and happiness is passing on smiles to other people. Try spending thirty minutes smiling at everyone you come into contact with. I have to put a caveat here that I am just talking a simple smile (you don't want to appear threatening).

I must confess that last time I did this exercise (not wanting to be judgemental) one of the people I smiled at had tattoos on his neck and face and he did shout "What the f*** are you looking at".

I would propose that you may want to ensure you carry out this exercise in a safe environment (at work etc.) or avoid people you don't feel comfortable creating eye contact with.

I could have I focused on the negative aspect of the one person who was threatening to me but ninety percent of the people did smile back at me. I chose to focus on the positive feedback as this enhanced my energy and helped me vibrate positively.

However you connect with others, I encourage you to focus on the benefits that these interactions give you.

Below is a list of the statements that I use to reaffirm what I have to be grateful for in this area:

HOW TO EXERCISE YOUR GRATITUDE MUSCLES

- I am happy and grateful that I can spread smiles and elicit positive feedback for myself as this raises my own happiness.
- I am happy and grateful that I have positive interactions with my work colleagues as it feeds my spirit.
- I am happy and grateful that my everyday interactions with others are primarily positive.
- I am happy and grateful that everyone I ever meet will know something I don't, as this means I can learn something from every interaction.
- I am happy and grateful that I work with a great team as having a strong team supports me in my activities and goals.
- I'm am happy and grateful that other people have different opinions to me as these diverse opinions help me grow as a person.
- I'm am happy and grateful that with over seven billion people on the planet there are always new people to meet, as new encounters bring new opportunities.

Exercise 33   Casual Acquaintances

I invite you now to complete at least one personal statement in this area that resonates with you. You can utilize part or all of any of the statements above or use something more personal to yourself.

*I am happy and grateful that*_____

_____

GRATITUDE FOR HAPPINESS

HOW TO EXERCISE YOUR GRATITUDE MUSCLES

Chapter Five   Material Possessions & Services

In the material world that most of us live in it can be seen as a badge of honour to accumulate the biggest and best possessions. Having the most stuff isn't always the answer. We've all heard tales of people who are extremely rich and still unhappy.

One man's opulence is another man's poverty so it is more how we feel about something than the actual financial value that allows us to be grateful for it.

This chapter is not about examining the levels of your current accumulations or your future goals but more about looking at what you have to be grateful for.

Growing up in Northern England I spent my childhood in an old Yorkshire stone house. I have to admit that the ice on the inside of the bedroom windows wouldn't be out of place on the watchers ice wall in "Game of Thrones". When you are raised with a poverty mentality it is very easy to accumulate too much stuff or to believe that you don't deserve extravagance or rich surroundings.

> *"True love is not in possessions or obsessions; it is in appreciation"* – **Debasish Mridha**

This chapter covers two main subjects: what we own (possessions) and what is provided for us (services).

I have divided the possessions area into necessities and luxuries as I believe this is a useful distinction. You can focus on the necessities you are grateful for before progressing to luxuries.

The items themselves are not as important as the emotions that they invoke in us. There are almost seventy example statements in this chapter – this is usually one of the easiest subjects for gratitude as the modern world provides us with so much to be grateful for.

1. Physical Necessities

Some people are wealthy and others have come from abject poverty so everyone's needs will be different. If we measure our basic needs only using a gauge such as "Maslow's hierarchy of needs", some of the items on your necessity list may seem like luxuries on the lists of others (and vice versa).

When I'm classifying something as a necessity or luxury I consider questions such as, "how many pairs of shoes can I wear at one time?"

However you decide which category to place your items in, remember it's you choice so if you find a statement below that you want to switch between the categories, feel free.

Below is a list of the statements that I use to reaffirm what I have to be grateful for in this area:

- I am happy and grateful that I realize that possessions are just stuff, and that by being unattached to possessions I need minimal stuff to be happy.
- I am happy and grateful that I have a waterproof jacket as it helps to keep me dry in the rain.
- I am happy and grateful that I have warm clothing to protect me in the cold weather.
- I am happy and grateful that I have a roof over my head that protects me from the elements.

HOW TO EXERCISE YOUR GRATITUDE MUSCLES

- I am happy and grateful that I have a nice warm bed to sleep in as it provides me a restful night's sleep.
- I am happy and grateful that I have a wood fire to heat my house as it makes the house so cosy.
- I am happy and grateful that I have a wetback boiler attached to my wood fire as it provides me free hot water in winter.
- I am happy and grateful that I have sturdy footwear to keep my feet dry in the rain.
- I am happy and grateful that I have food in my cupboards and my freezer as food keeps me alive.
- I am happy and grateful that I have a large pile of firewood to keep me warm through the winter.
- I am happy and grateful that I always have enough food to eat every day.
- I am happy and grateful that I have curtains and blinds on the windows to keep out the light on a summer's morning.
- I am happy and grateful that I have a landline telephone as it allows me to keep me in contact with my elderly mother overseas.
- I am happy and grateful that the modern world in which I live provides me with things now classed as standard that were previously classed as luxurious, as this reminds me how great our current lives are.
- I am happy and grateful that I always have a pen or a way of taking notes as once I have an idea written down it frees up my brain for the next idea.

Exercise 34   Physical Necessities

I invite you now to complete at least one personal statement in this area that resonates with you. You can utilize part or all of any of the statements above or use something more personal to yourself.

GRATITUDE FOR HAPPINESS

*I am happy and grateful that*_____

_____

2. Physical Luxuries

As I stated above, classing something as a luxury can be subjective and when we grade something as a luxury it can actually bring up emotions of guilt and anguish within us.

> *"The best and most beautiful things in the world cannot be seen or even touched, they must be felt with the heart"*
> — **Helen Keller**

I encourage you to allow yourself to deserve the odd luxury. A little bit of indulgence once in a while can actually aid your emotional wellness.

Whether your idea of luxury is a hot cup of coffee on a Sunday morning or a weekend getaway on a private yacht, you should not judge your decisions too harshly. Be kind to yourself.

Below is a list of the statements that I use to reaffirm what I have to be grateful for in this area:

- I am happy and grateful that I have a mobile phone that allows me to keep in contact with my friends and family.
- I am happy and grateful that my accommodation has a serviceable bathroom close at hand so that I can go to the toilet in comfort whenever I want.

HOW TO EXERCISE YOUR GRATITUDE MUSCLES

- I am happy and grateful that I have a great shampoo as it helps to keep my dandruff under control.
- I am happy and grateful that I own a serviceable car so that I can travel when I want to.
- I am happy and grateful that I have access to YouTube and the connection it provides me to the world.
- I am happy and grateful that I have two bathrooms as it enhances visits when friends stay.
- I am happy and grateful that I have an abundance of clothes as it allows me choices.
- I am happy and grateful that I have reading spectacles as they allow me to read.
- I am happy and grateful that I have a laptop computer as it allows me to write articles, letters and books.
- I am happy and grateful that I have large bath towels as they make drying after a bath or shower so much easier.
- I am happy and grateful that I have motivational quotes situated around my house as they help to feed my soul.
- I am happy and grateful that I have an automatic washing machine as it allows me a constant supply of clean clothes.
- I am happy and grateful that I have access to deodorants and aftershave as they enhance my hygiene regime.
- I am happy and grateful that I have a kindle digital reader as it allows me to carry lots of books and keep the knowledge readily available.

Exercise 35   Physical Luxuries

I invite you now to complete at least one personal statement in this area that resonates with you. You can utilize part or all of any of the statements above or use something more personal to yourself.

GRATITUDE FOR HAPPINESS

*I am happy and grateful that*_____

_____

3. Physical Luxuries continued
- I am happy and grateful that I have access to healthy foods that provide fuel for my body.
- I am happy and grateful that I can attend cinemas as they provide me some pleasant escapism.
- I am happy and grateful that I have a great book collection as it allows me to learn from others works.
- I am happy and grateful that I have toothpaste as it protects my teeth, making my mouth clean and fresh.
- I am happy and grateful that I have a working car stereo as it turns my car into both a university and a disco.
- I am happy and grateful that I have an electric kettle as it provides me near instant hot water.
- I am happy and grateful that I have a smartphone as it is useful for both work and play.
- I am happy and grateful that I have a garage to keep my car in as it allows for clear windscreens on winter's mornings.
- I am happy and grateful that I have my own hair clippers as they allow me to have a haircut at short notice.
- I am happy and grateful that I have soft toilet paper as it is very kind to my bottom.
- I am happy and grateful that I have moisturizing cream as it salves and protects the cracked skin of my heels.
- I am happy and grateful that I have pictures of cute animals as I get the benefits of looking at animals without the responsibilities.

- I am happy and grateful that I have after sun lotion in the bathroom as it soothes my skin when I'm sunburnt.
- I am happy and grateful that pharmacies sell soft paper handkerchiefs infused with Aloe Vera as they are kind to my nose when I have a cold.
- I am happy and grateful that I have a microwave oven as it makes food preparation so quick and easy.
- I am happy and grateful that I have my pole chainsaw as it makes the trimming of high hedges easier.
- I am happy and grateful that I have multiple sets of bedding so that I can always have clean bedding to maintain my hygiene.
- I am happy and grateful that I have international spices readily available as they add flavour to a bland dish and enhance my meals.
- I am happy and grateful that I have a laminator as this allows me to protect cards and posters to help me keep focused on my positivity.

Exercise 36   Physical Luxuries Continued

I invite you now to complete at least one personal statement in this area that resonates with you. You can utilize part or all of any of the statements above or use something more personal to yourself.

*I am happy and grateful that*_____

_____

4. Available Services

Physical belongings tend to be the things that we focus on when referring to possessions but if we are going to talk about luxuries we need to include non-physical pleasures.

In this instance, when we are classifying something as a service we can be referring to a literal service from a person such as a cleaning lady or store assistant or the bounty from a tree in our garden.

You will be pleasantly surprised when you start to search at how many of these services are available to you. By exhibiting gratitude for these services you will attract even more.

Below is a list of the statements that I use to reaffirm what I have to be grateful for in this area:

- I am happy and grateful that I have access to music as it fills my heart and my soul.
- I am happy and grateful that I have electric lighting as it provides me instant light in the dark.
- I am happy and grateful that I am able to utilize the skills of virtual assistants and others so that I can maximize the use of my own time.
- I am happy and grateful that I have access to modern technology that allows me to launch books.
- I am happy and grateful that I have access to the retail industry as it allows me to make so many purchases, with multiple items readily at hand.
- I am happy and grateful that there are farmers who produce food as this makes sustenance readily available to me.
- I am happy and grateful that my freezer includes an ice maker as this ensures ice is readily available on hot days.

- I am happy and grateful that I have a Thai chilli plant as it provides a bounty of free chillies for my cooking.
- I am happy and grateful that some weekend courses provide catering for the whole weekend as this allows me to focus on the course content rather than on what I'm going to eat.
- I am happy and grateful that motels provide tea making equipment, comfy beds and private bathrooms as this provides me all that I need close at hand.

Exercise 37   Available Services

I invite you now to complete at least one personal statement in this area that resonates with you. You can utilize part or all of any of the statements above or use something more personal to yourself.

*I am happy and grateful that*_____

_____

5. Available Services continued
- I am happy and grateful that there is so much useful information available online as it helps to estimate and create projections for the success of a venture prior to investments.
- I am happy and grateful that a good night's sleep, a meal and a shower can recharge my batteries as these are usually readily available.
- I am happy and grateful that some motels provide fresh coffee in the rooms as it wakes me up in a morning.
- I am happy and grateful that my word processing software has a thesaurus as this allows me to quickly build the vocabulary in my documents.

GRATITUDE FOR HAPPINESS

- I am happy and grateful for the availability of British comedy as it matches my sense of humour and adds to the happiness in my life.
- I am happy and grateful that my phone has a voice recorder function as it helps me take notes legibly and fast enough to keep up with my brain.
- I am happy and grateful that I have electricity available at the flick of a switch as the benefits this provides make my life much more pleasurable.
- I am happy and grateful that I can access the information left by previous generations so that I can speed up my own learnings and project advancements.
- I am happy and grateful that I have access to international banks as they allow me access to funds worldwide.

Exercise 38   Available Services continued

I invite you now to complete at least one personal statement in this area that resonates with you. You can utilize part or all of any of the statements above or use something more personal to yourself.

*I am happy and grateful that*_____

_____

HOW TO EXERCISE YOUR GRATITUDE MUSCLES

Chapter Six — Careers & Skills

No matter how long we live, we are influenced by events from our upbringing and our childhood.

Although this influence can be positive, a lot of us are moulded by the negative aspects of our beginnings (a poverty mentality etc.) and this can make it difficult for us to achieve success in our lives.

Whether we start out with a paper round after school or part time bar work to get us through college, we can start to develop positive skills and coping methods from a very early age.

In this chapter we are going to look at the areas of your life relating to work, careers and the skills that you have developed that can enhance your life and happiness.

Most people do not realize how talented they are until they examine themselves. I encourage you to dig deep to draw as many positive aspects from past your journey as you can.

1. Careers

Only a few years ago, when people left school or college they started along a career journey that was reasonably well structured. Most people stayed in the same industries until retiring and there was very little chance for advancement.

Modern technology and the opportunities today's global community provides us mean that we now have many more alternatives.

Whether you are looking at the lifestyle of a travelling entrepreneur, becoming a leader of industry or running a home based business, there will be lots of opportunities for gratitude along the way.

You may be reading this section at the start of your working career or you may be at some other stage along your career path. If you look deep enough at your own situation you will find that there is always something to be grateful for.

Below is a list of the statements that I use to reaffirm what I have to be grateful for in this area:

- I am happy and grateful that I started a paper round and then a part time job while I was still at school as this instilled in me a great work ethic for my future careers.
- I am happy and grateful that I quit the corporate world and decided to become an entrepreneur as it set me free.
- I am happy and grateful that I have been able to have multiple careers during my life. This was due to my personal choices and has lead me to my current situation.
- I am happy and grateful that working from home means I don't need to leave the house on a frosty morning as I prefer not to venture out into hazardous conditions.
- I am happy and grateful that I have access to the opportunities to build online businesses as this allows career flexibility on an international scale.
- I am happy and grateful that I was able to progress through the rank system in the British military as this allowed me a fruitful military career.
- I am happy and grateful that I was able to utilize my management and construction skills in the reconstruction of post-earthquake Canterbury New Zealand.

- I am happy and grateful that the promotions I earned throughout my career have allowed me to fund a better quality of life.

Exercise 39   Careers

I invite you now to complete at least one personal statement in this area that resonates with you. You can utilize part or all of any of the statements above or use something more personal to yourself.

*I am happy and grateful that*_____

_____

2. Education

There is a lot of debate as to the benefits of a formal education as opposed to other skill development. I'm a firm believer in the need for the basics. When I was a child we used to have the catchy title of the three R's (Reading, Righting & Rithmatic) to represent reading, writing and arithmetic. However the basics are classified, numerical and textual literacy are something I believe are a must.

> *"Formal education will make you a living; self-education will make you a fortune"* – **Jim Rohn.**

In some countries there is a recognized path to higher education resulting in lots of highly qualified people with qualifications they cannot use. I am not wishing to debate which is the right path to success. I am aiming to get you to focus on any particular strengths and achievements you have accrued on your personal path.

You are probably not aware how many skills and talents you have. There are many cases of success and wealth in people without a formal education, so ensure you look closely at what you have learned along the way when you are formulating your gratitude.

Below is a list of the statements that I use to reaffirm what I have to be grateful for in this area:

- I am happy and grateful that I have the ability to read as it helps to keep me up to date in new advancements in life.
- I am happy and grateful that I learned to count as this basic skill has helped me in so many areas of my life.
- I am happy and grateful that I was a so-called geek at school as the continued pursuit of my passion to learn has served me well throughout my life.
- I am happy and grateful that I received a public education as a child because it has helped me survive, progress and thrive throughout life.
- I am happy and grateful that I don't have the answer to every question as the search for answers is the fun bit.
- I am happy and grateful that I recently achieved a project management diploma as it shows I can still gain qualifications later in life.
- I am happy and grateful that I have accomplished so much in my life as this has given me purpose.
- I am happy and grateful that I start each day with a thirst for knowledge as this drives me to ask the question, "what am I going to learn today to benefit me?"

- I am happy and grateful that I succeeded in gaining an Honours degree in environmental science as it showed me that I am capable of completing higher education.
- I am happy and grateful that I have the ability to learn new subjects quickly as this helps me to adapt to new challenges.

Exercise 40   Education

I invite you now to complete at least one personal statement in this area that resonates with you. You can utilize part or all of any of the statements above or use something more personal to yourself.

*I am happy and grateful that*_____

_____

3. Progress

When we are building our skills and learning our trades, it is important that we enjoy the journey rather than just focusing on the end goals.

Like most people I am conscious of marking progress in different ventures. Whether it is an assignment for a qualification, financial progress for a business, the amount written for a book or something as simple as the preparation of a meal, we all tend to measure progress against some metric. The metric can be time, money, number of words or any other measure of progress.

> *"It does not matter how slowly you go as long as you do not stop"* – **Confucius**

HOW TO EXERCISE YOUR GRATITUDE MUSCLES

We gauge our success against our own specific scale and if we haven't achieved our goals we are tempted to berate ourselves.

Celebrating small wins along our journey allows us to focus on positivity rather than a lack of achievement. In this section I encourage you to look at any and all progress you have made and celebrate it with gratitude.

Below is a list of the statements that I use to reaffirm what I have to be grateful for in this area:

- I am happy and grateful that I have completed the enrolment forms for my degree course as this is the first step to achieving my degree.
- I am happy and grateful that I purchased a book on personal development today as this is the first step on the journey.
- I am happy and grateful that every word, sentence, paragraph or page that I complete in an assignment, book or venture is progress towards a goal.
- I am happy and grateful that I can immerse myself in new subjects and pick up new skills quickly as this allows me to succeed in new adventures.
- I am happy and grateful that I have a set of written goals so that I know where I'm going in life and can monitor my progress.
- I am happy and grateful that I have a competitive nature as it drives me to thrive.
- I am happy and grateful that I have already created almost half of the content for my project as progress initiates more progress.

- I am happy and grateful that when I finish a project I can remain detached as it allows me to quickly move on to the next opportunity in my life.
- I am happy and grateful that I have written a whole paragraph of my book today as that is one paragraph closer to completing this book.

Exercise 41   Progress

I invite you now to complete at least one personal statement in this area that resonates with you. You can utilize part or all of any of the statements above or use something more personal to yourself.

*I am happy and grateful that*_____

_____

4. Creativity

We tend to believe that we are either creative or not. We may see ourselves as being able to build computer apps, design amazing buildings or be destined to only dig a hole with a shovel.

As an ex-soldier I must admit that I had a history of not classing myself as creative. A few years ago, if someone had mentioned a creative type, I envisaged (and envied) an artistic, imaginative person who was more about music and the arts than a manual worker.

It's taken me several years of attempting new activities such as African & Egyptian drumming and various forms of dancing to get out of my comfort zone, but that seems to have cultivated my creative muscles more. Although I am not siting any scientific evidence in this book, there is plenty of information out there that supports the theory that creativity can be learned.

I myself have noticed an improvement in my own creativity and would encourage others to experiment in this area. What we focus on is what we attract and I firmly believe that focusing on creative activities has helped my creative muscles grow.

I encourage you to celebrate your creativity and be grateful for all of those qualities.

Below is a list of the statements that I use to reaffirm what I have to be grateful for in this area:

- I am happy and grateful that I sang in a choir as a child as it helped to grow my singing voice.
- I am happy and grateful that I have published two books in the last eight months as it has proven to me that I can be more creative.
- I am happy and grateful that I took up African drumming and then Egyptian drumming as they showed me that I have a creative side.
- I am happy and grateful that I know how to use hand tools as this allows me to make and fix things.
- I am happy and grateful that I am ready to write as soon as I wake up as this allows me to document the thoughts that my subconscious mind produces whilst I am sleeping.
- I am happy and grateful that I have learned to dance as it helps me express myself.
- I am happy and grateful that I have a background in engineering as it helps me to solve problems.
- I am happy and grateful that every situation in my life gives me potential material for books as we all have at least one

book in us and continually collecting material makes writing a book easier.
- I am happy and grateful that I am able to create a mass of content and then organize it into a structured book as this has helped me to utilize my structured thought process whilst also being creative.
- I am happy and grateful that I have developed my creative side as it has allowed me to achieve things I never thought possible.
- I am happy and grateful that I have experienced the process of writing a book and seeing it develop as this is an interesting process that adds quality to my life.

Exercise 42   Creativity

I invite you now to complete at least one personal statement in this area that resonates with you. You can utilize part or all of any of the statements above or use something more personal to yourself.

*I am happy and grateful that*_____

_____

5. Self Confidence

Achieving any level of self-confidence can be judged as a skill but we tend to judge ourselves against too high a standard. Getting out of bed in the morning can be a challenge for some people so don't feel that you need to become an international speaker (unless you want to) and stand up in front of thousands of people to prove your self-confidence.

HOW TO EXERCISE YOUR GRATITUDE MUSCLES

Begin by focusing on the small items of your confidence – even something as simple as being grateful for choosing a new hair cut is a start.

We all have some level of self-confidence and I encourage you to celebrate yours. Be grateful for what you have and you will attract more of the same.

Below is a list of the statements that I use to reaffirm what I have to be grateful for in this area:

- I am happy and grateful that I have the self-confidence to leave the house every day.
- I am happy and grateful that I feel no requirement to dye my grey hairs as I believe that they are distinguishing.
- I am happy and grateful that I can control the amount of alcohol I drink as it allows me the choice to maintain cognisance and also to relax.
- I am happy and grateful that I have the confidence to back myself in ventures, as I believe if nothing is ventured then nothing is gained.
- I am happy and grateful that I have the self-confidence to produce YouTube videos of myself and put myself out there for perpetuity. It keeps me genuine and reinforces being comfortable in my own skin.
- I am happy and grateful that I am happy in my own skin, as it's taken me years to become who I am; I choose to celebrate that person.
- I am happy and grateful that I am responsible for my own destiny as it enables me to take responsibility for my actions.
- I am happy and grateful that I am comfortable in reasonably priced clothes as I am not defined by other people's values.

- I am happy and grateful that I am able to say "NO" to things that are not a priority to me, as being happy is governed more by what we say "No" to than what we say "Yes" to.
- I am happy and grateful that I have a level of self-confidence that is not hubris. By being happy but not arrogant this allows me balance in my life.
- I am happy and grateful that I understand that my failures are not permanent as I can always start over again.

Exercise 43   Self Confidence

I invite you now to complete at least one personal statement in this area that resonates with you. You can utilize part or all of any of the statements above or use something more personal to yourself.

*I am happy and grateful that*_____

_____

6. Personal Development

I am assuming that as you purchased this book you are interested in subjects that will enhance you personally. Working on improving ourselves in any area is a great idea and picking up a book or audio course is a popular way to enter into the personal development field.

Celebrating even the first steps on your journey can help speed up your progress to the next stage of your development.

HOW TO EXERCISE YOUR GRATITUDE MUSCLES

"It's never too late – never too late to start over, never too late to be happy" – **Jane Fonda**

I remember that one of the first personal development books I purchased was Robert Kiyosaki's "Rich Dad Poor Dad". I was on my first trip to New Zealand and someone suggested it to me. I bought it in Singapore airport on my way back to Cyprus and finished it before the plane landed in Greece.

That one book started me on a journey that I expect to be on until the day I die, so I am grateful for the recommendation and where it has led me.

Feel free to log and to celebrate all of the steps on your journey, big or small.

Below is a list of the statements that I use to reaffirm what I have to be grateful for in this area:

- I am happy and grateful that someone recommended the book "Rich Dad Poor Dad" to me as it started me on an amazing journey.
- I am happy and grateful that I have undertaken DISC profile testing as it helped me paint a better picture of myself.
- I am happy and grateful that I found mentors who suited me for my trading education.
- I am happy and grateful that I am continually developing skills to improve who I am as we can always improve who we are.
- I am happy and grateful that even the smallest improvement in myself is a step in the right direction and so should be celebrated.

- I am happy and grateful that I have had such rich and varied life experiences as they have helped mould me into the person I am.
- I am happy and grateful that I took action and invested my time in a business start-up weekend as action is a choice and there are always alternatives.
- I am happy and grateful that I can acknowledge all of the moments of my own personal growth as this motivates me for further growth.

Exercise 44   Personal Development

I invite you now to complete at least one personal statement in this area that resonates with you. You can utilize part or all of any of the statements above or use something more personal to yourself.

*I am happy and grateful that*_____

_____

7. General Skills

Whenever we refer to skills we tend to consider activities that can be used to advance our careers or vocations. It can be easy to overlook the general everyday competences that we pick up along the way.

Acknowledging even your smallest of talent allows you to stretch those gratitude muscles and observe your bigger achievements.

HOW TO EXERCISE YOUR GRATITUDE MUSCLES

"You only live once, but if you do it right, once is enough" – **Mae West**

Remember that no object of your gratitude is too small and if you can find lots of small things to be grateful for you will soon advance to bigger things.

Below is a list of the statements that I use to reaffirm what I have to be grateful for in this area:

- I am happy and grateful that I passed my vehicle driving licence as this has given me huge amounts of freedom over the years.
- I am happy and grateful that I can cook as it allows me to prepare yummy treats.
- I am happy and grateful that I am goal driven as this has helped me to succeed in past ventures.
- I am happy and grateful that I have a systematic outlook as it stops me being overwhelmed in complex situations.
- I am happy and grateful that I learned to iron my clothing so that I can look good on special occasions.
- I am happy and grateful that I have developed patience as it has helped me avoid stress in my life.
- I am happy and grateful that can I make packing lists as they ensure I have what I need when travelling.
- I am happy and grateful that I am able to bake as it is therapeutic and helps support my love language of giving by giving most of it away.
- I am happy and grateful that I start every day with a blank canvas and the ability to write my own story.

GRATITUDE FOR HAPPINESS

- I am happy and grateful that I am able to identify small issues before they grow out of control as catching something when it is still manageable avoids disasters.
- I am happy and grateful that I remember to compile a shopping list before going shopping as it helps avoid cluttering and unnecessary expense.
- I am happy and grateful that I don't sweat the small stuff as it makes my life a lot happier.
- I am happy and grateful that I learned to shave my facial hair as it makes me feel fresher.
- I am happy and grateful that I can wake up naturally without an alarm clock as it allows me to ease into the day stress free.
- I am happy and grateful that I have a flexible outlook on life as it allows me to adapt to different situations.
- I am happy and grateful that I have the commitment to complete a thirty day course as knowing that I can complete one course helps me commit to starting other courses.
- I am happy and grateful that I can wake up by the light of the sun as this simple thing helps me wake up refreshed.

Exercise 45   General Skills

I invite you now to complete at least one personal statement in this area that resonates with you. You can utilize part or all of any of the statements above or use something more personal to yourself.

*I am happy and grateful that*_____

_____

8. Our Own Success

We tend to gauge our success by comparing ourselves to others through either monetary or other standards of wealth. Even the richest people on earth may feel that they are not yet successful as it is their own individual benchmarks that they judge this by.

You can still be happy if you aren't the richest person on earth as long as you feel successful and one way of reaffirming your success is to be grateful for what you have already achieved.

> *"Success is not final, failure is not fatal, it is the courage to continue that counts"* – **Winston Churchill**

I encourage you to celebrate whatever level of success you have currently achieved and remember to enjoy the journey to greater success rather than just waiting to reach your destination.

Below is a list of the statements that I use to reaffirm what I have to be grateful for in this area:

- I am happy and grateful that I have failed regularly as the lessons the failures have taught me have helped me succeed.
- I am happy and grateful that I can tick off just one item on my to do list as every item gives me a sense of achievement.
- I am happy and grateful that my persistence is building my success as this provides me hope.
- I am happy and grateful that by setting my monthly goals at the start of the month it helps me to achieve them by the end of the month, as this reaffirms to me that goal setting helps with my success.

- I am happy and grateful that I wake up every day buzzing with ideas of things to do that day as this adds to both my motivation to succeed and my happiness.
- I am happy and grateful that my second book's sales were not very strong as this provided me many learnings for my next book to succeed.
- I am happy and grateful that I achieved the top seven percent of the people who publish a book by selling more than five hundred copies.

Exercise 46   Our Own Success

I invite you now to complete at least one personal statement in this area that resonates with you. You can utilize part or all of any of the statements above or use something more personal to yourself.

*I am happy and grateful that*_____

_____

9. The Success of Others

Studies have shown that a majority of people would rather have a lesser pay rise if it meant that they would still earn more than their colleagues. E.g. A person would rather have a personal 15% pay rise if their co-workers received a 10% pay rise than receive a personal 20% pay rise if their co-workers received a 25% pay rise.

Think about that for a minute. People would rather get less money themselves as long as they got more than others.

HOW TO EXERCISE YOUR GRATITUDE MUSCLES

Perhaps it is because the majority of people are trying to keep up with the Joneses that they do not succeed as much as the minority of people who think differently.

> *"There are two ways of spreading light: to be the candle or the mirror that reflects it"* — **Edith Wharton**

Focus on everyone succeeding and this will help you with an abundance mentality.

I firmly believe that celebrating the success of others can help attract success to yourself as it helps you vibrate at a higher level.

Below is a list of the statements that I use to reaffirm what I have to be grateful for in this area:

- I am happy and grateful that my friends are having success in their endeavours as this inspires me to succeed.
- I am happy and grateful that I can use the success of international writers and mentors to inspire me to succeed.
- I am happy and grateful that the success of para Olympians drives me to push my body physically.
- I am happy and grateful that following Tim Ferris's success technique of batch checking emails has helped with my time management success.
- I am happy and grateful that I can produce books that benefit others and help them succeed because contributing to others reinforces my happiness and also benefits me financially.
- I am happy and grateful that I have built a free online course that requires no further input from me as it can continue

contributing to others' success whilst leaving me time to devote to other ventures.
- I am happy and grateful that I have begun a series of beginner's guide books as each book allows me to build on the previous book and help even more people succeed.

Exercise 47   The Success of Others
I invite you now to complete at least one personal statement in this area that resonates with you. You can utilize part or all of any of the statements above or use something more personal to yourself.

*I am happy and grateful that*_____

_____

HOW TO EXERCISE YOUR GRATITUDE MUSCLES

Chapter Seven   Time

At some stage during our day, week or month we can have the feeling that there isn't enough time. We all have the same twenty-four hours in each day yet we have different perceptions of lack or abundance depending on our assessment of that time.

> *"I'm so busy I don't know if I found a rope or lost my horse"* –
> **Mark Schafer**

There are times in our life when we feel that we are not in charge of our own schedule. When someone suggest that all we need to do is get up earlier or put aside time for activities, we feel that they just don't understand how busy we are!

I can relate to feeling time poor as not long after I moved to New Zealand I found myself working three jobs. Juggling three jobs meant that my midweek schedule was pretty crowded.

I used to go to work at ten p.m. Wednesday nights and work in a petrol service station until seven a.m. on Thursday morning. Thursday daytime would be spent trading options on the Australian stock exchange and sometimes I would manage a multi-level marketing presentation before starting another night shift at eight pm back at the petrol station. This meant that if I was lucky I would manage a couple of hours sleep during a period of over thirty-six hours.

Many of the people reading this book may have pushed their schedules in a similar way to me, but that kind of life is not sustainable (or actually a life!).

HOW TO EXERCISE YOUR GRATITUDE MUSCLES

I include my example purely to show that I understand your time can be precious, but if you focus on the positives and are grateful for the bounty they bring, it can help promote your happiness.

> *"Your time on earth is limited so don't waste it living somebody else's life"* – **Steve Jobs**

As we start to get a little older we may feel that we have used up (or wasted) most of our lifespan. A lot of this is determined by our own view of events. Whether you are a "glass half full" or a "glass half empty" type of person can establish your own perception of exactly the same results.

1. Prioritization

We all have exactly the same twenty-four hours in our day so how we prioritize those hours can determine not just our success but our happiness.

You may choose to switch a work shift with a colleague so that you can experience an event in one of your family's life, or choose to miss out on an annual vacation day so that you can have a better holiday at a later time.

During the early years of our life we may choose to spend our college nights studying, working on future businesses or drinking with our friends. Determining that you are in charge of your time is one of the first steps to happiness.

Being grateful for the ability to determine how you spend your days allows you to focus on the positives of your situation and grow your happiness.

GRATITUDE FOR HAPPINESS

Below is a list of the statements that I use to reaffirm what I have to be grateful for in this area:

- I am happy and grateful that I have enough sleep each night as this enables me to recharge my energy levels.
- I am happy and grateful that after working a long night shift I get to watch the sunrise and it reinvigorates me.
- I am happy and grateful that I can always set aside time to exercise as it is a priority for my health.
- I am happy and grateful that I can always eat my food at a leisurely pace as this aids my digestion.
- I am happy and grateful that I have the flexibility in my schedule to facilitate emergencies as we all need contingencies.
- I am happy and grateful that when I need to drop someone off early at the airport it allows me to start my day earlier and achieve more.
- I am happy and grateful that I have sufficient time available for the important things in my life.
- I am happy and grateful that I can delay answering texts and phone calls as this allows me to control my own schedule.
- I am happy and grateful that I can choose not to answer emails first thing in the morning as this allows me to work to prioritize my schedule and not have to work to someone else's timetable.
- I am happy and grateful that I have the capability to commit to a thirty day plan and stick to the activities as this allows me to maximize my results and is a great investment of my time.
- I am happy and grateful that I have an engine powered lawn mower as it reduces the time I need to allocate to mowing my lawns.

HOW TO EXERCISE YOUR GRATITUDE MUSCLES

Exercise 48   Prioritization

I invite you now to complete at least one personal statement in this area that resonates with you. You can utilize part or all of any of the statements above or use something more personal to yourself.

*I am happy and grateful that*_____

_____

2. Perception

We tend to feel that time drags when we are doing unpleasant tasks and it speeds up during our pleasurable times. It is the same twenty-four hours no matter how you perceive it but by using that time in ways that benefit you (both physically and mentally) it will add quality to your life.

I have to confess that my skype calls to my family overseas feel like I've been talking for ten minutes when in effect they have gone on for over an hour.

Before you read any further in this section I want you to draw your mind back to a time when you did an activity that seemed to drag on (such as an exam that you didn't know any of the answers.) and another time where your activity was so enthralling that time seemed to fly.

"Put your hand on a hot stove for a minute, and it seems like an hour. Sit with a pretty girl for an hour and it seems like a minute"
*– **Albert Einstein***

GRATITUDE FOR HAPPINESS

Harness your memories and be grateful that you have all of the time in the world.

Below is a list of the statements that I use to reaffirm what I have to be grateful for in this area:

- I am happy and grateful that my wedding day seemed to pass in slow time as there were so many amazing moments to savour.
- I am happy and grateful that I invest the first five minutes after I awake each day in a state of meditation as this clears my mind and gives me the feeling that I have lots of time available for my tasks.
- I am happy and grateful that I have learned to divide my tasks into chunks as by having a large number of achievable goals each day I feel as though I have completed twice as much work and this is great for my confidence.
- I am happy and grateful that I have work that I enjoy as rather than watching the clock I get lost in my work and the result is increased productivity.
- I am happy and grateful that whenever I get up early to drop someone at the airport it allows me to start work earlier. Starting work earlier gives me a perception of productivity at an earlier time in the day which becomes a self-fulfilling prophecy.
- I am happy and grateful that I am able to mentally pause when I have an impending deadline for a task as this pause allows me to assess my options and maximize the use of my time.

Exercise 49   Perception

I invite you now to complete at least one personal statement in this area that resonates with you. You can utilize part or all of any

of the statements above or use something more personal to yourself.

*I am happy and grateful that*_____

_____

3. Delays

If you have you ever been stressed out about missing an appointment or a plane, you need to realize that you can glean something positive from every situation depending on how you view it.

There are plenty of documented cases where being late or absent from your normal routine has been beneficial. Several people (such as the actor Seth MacFarlane) were scheduled to fly on one of the planes that were crashed on 9/11, but their plans changed so they weren't there. Some people late for work that day also avoided being in the towers when they fell.

I myself was recently booked to fly from Australia to New Zealand and the flight was delayed a couple of hours. When I went to the airline booking desk to check in the attendant gave me a food and drink voucher and when I started smiling she said "You're the only person who seems happy that this flight was delayed". She had apparently been given a hard time by some passengers but I pointed out that I was ex-military and over the years I had flights that were delayed for days rather than hours.

My previous delays had entailed sitting in locations such as tents in the desert with nothing to do whereas in this situation I had my iPad loaded with books and films plus I was being supplied a free meal and a drink.

GRATITUDE FOR HAPPINESS

"The greatest remedy for anger is delay" – **Thomas Paine**

Next time you miss an appointment or experience some kind of delay, be grateful for the potential positive outcomes that it presents to you.

Below is a list of the statements that I use to reaffirm what I have to be grateful for in this area:

- I am happy and grateful that I always have an activity planned in case of a flight delay as this has reduced the stress in my life.
- I am happy and grateful that Singapore Airlines supply a free hotel room if my flights are delayed a few hours, as this breaks up the journey.
- I am happy and grateful that I once missed a flight to Canada as it has ensured that I always allow extra time to get to the airport and I have always been on time for flights since.
- I am happy and grateful that I was late for work today as I am free to work more time after my colleagues have gone home. Solitary work makes me more productive and centred.
- I am happy and grateful that the police officer pulled me over for speeding as I avoided a collision that occurred on the road in front of me.
- I am happy and grateful that I receive a free meal voucher if my flights are delayed from Australia.

Exercise 50   Delays

I invite you now to complete at least one personal statement in this area that resonates with you. You can utilize part or all of any of the statements above or use something more personal to yourself.

*I am happy and grateful that*_____
_____

GRATITUDE FOR HAPPINESS

Chapter Eight   Passions & Contributions

There is a theory that most wealthy entrepreneurs are philanthropic because they are passionate about their contribution to society as well as their own wellbeing.

Being passionate and contributing are not attributes that are limited to the wealthy few as we all have those potentials within us.

I would class myself as a passionate person in that I throw my energy into ventures with all of my heart and soul, but I do not feel restricted to having only one passion.

Whether you are passionate about creating art masterpieces, watching Formula One racing or funding charities, these are all activities that can promote positive emotions within you.

I encourage you to embrace your passions and be grateful that you can choose the activities that create your happiness.

"For the past 33 years I have looked in the mirror every morning and asked myself,

'If today was the last day of my life, would I want to do what I am about to do today?'

And whenever the answer has been 'No' for too many days in a row, I know I need to change something" – **Steve Jobs**

1. Passion

As we move through life we may be the kind of person who finds their one true passion and commits to that wholly throughout our lives. I offer my respect to these individuals as these fortunate people are few and far between.

For the rest of us, we will spend our journey searching for areas to invest our energy. We may discard old passions and develop new ones but both old and new can add to the mix that make us who we are today.

> *"Don't be afraid your life will end; be afraid that it will never begin"* – **Grace Hansen**

The intensity with which we pursue these passions will to some extent determine our results and in that same way, the amount of energy we commit to our gratitude will also influence our results.

The mere word "passion" can invoke positive emotions in you so I encourage you to harness this energy when you are contemplating your gratitude statements in this area.

Below is a list of the statements that I use to reaffirm what I have to be grateful for in this area:

- I am happy and grateful that I can commit the same passion to building a business as I do to baking a cake as injecting passion into any venture produces stronger results.
- I am happy and grateful that as I progress through life trying new things they provide me with more to be grateful for and this then gives me the impetus to continually try new things.
- I am happy and grateful that I am passionate about words as just a few positive words or phrases can inspire happiness within me.

GRATITUDE FOR HAPPINESS

- I am happy and grateful that the mere sound of a song can arouse passion in me and raise my vibrations to new heights.
- I am happy and grateful that I can express my passions through my blog posts and enhance others' lives.
- I am happy and grateful that I have found some purpose in my life as it helps me to thrive.
- I am happy and grateful that I have lots of exciting opportunities coming my way as this gives me hope and lots to look forward to.

Exercise 51   Passion

I invite you now to complete at least one personal statement in this area that resonates with you. You can utilize part or all of any of the statements above or use something more personal to yourself.

*I am happy and grateful that*_____

_____

2. Sports & Pastimes

Whether you currently play sport, have retired or are just a spectator, this can be an area of your life that can give rise to obsession and other feelings. Even superstars have sub-par performances and if you or your team is going through a low spot you can choose to focus on the negatives or search for the positives of the situation.

I have on my bookshelf a runners-up medal from a Rugby Sevens tournament I competed in back in 1995. I could focus on the fact that I haven't played rugby for years or that we came second rather than winning but I choose to draw as many positives as possible from that experience.

Below is a list of the statements that I use to reaffirm what I have to be grateful for in this area:

- I am happy and grateful that I was in a runner-up team for a rugby tournament as coming second out of ten teams allowed me to experience victory and loss at the same time.
- I am happy and grateful that I learned to ride a horse as they are lovely animals that can provide both grounding and exhilaration.
- I am happy and grateful that my rugby team have won a game this season as they are clearly improving.
- I am happy and grateful that I have dual citizenship as it allows me to support multiple international sports teams at the same time.
- I am happy and grateful that I enjoyed cross country running as a child as it made my army basic training more enjoyable.
- I am happy and grateful that I played in sports teams as this has helped me learn how to interact with other people.
- I am happy and grateful that when I have played sport I know that I have given one hundred percent commitment as this helps to show me that I can provide this commitment to my other obligations in life.

Exercise 52   Sports & Pastimes

I invite you now to complete at least one personal statement in this area that resonates with you. You can utilize part or all of any of the statements above or use something more personal to yourself.

*I am happy and grateful that*_____

_____

3. Hobbies

It is said that the difference between a business and a hobby is that a business puts money in your pocket and a hobby takes money out of your pocket. The benefits of hobbies are not always visible to the naked eye and whether your hobby is racing super yachts or collecting the serial numbers of locomotives, the benefits you experience do not have to depend on the financial costs of the activity.

We should assume that you are taking part in a hobby because you enjoy it, so let's focus on the benefits that you enjoy from the hobby. Over the last year or so I have personally been receiving instruction in the art of Wing Chun and I ensure that I schedule some daily Wing Chun into my calendar. I could focus on the fact that this is a daily commitment but I prefer to focus on the benefits.

I encourage you to focus on the benefits that your hobbies are providing you and express gratitude for those benefits.

Below is a list of the statements that I use to reaffirm what I have to be grateful for in this area:

- I am happy and grateful that I discovered laughter yoga as it helped me survive some challenging times.
- I am happy and grateful that I am a Wing Chun practitioner as the practice helps me keep centred and exercises the joints that are normally weakened as we age.

- I am happy and grateful that I picked up archery quickly as it seems I have some natural ability in that area.
- I am happy and grateful that I have completed a one hour video recording of my first form of Wing Chun this has provided me a great reference resource if I ever have to break from my practice.
- I am happy and grateful that my mother learned to knit as it provided me so many jumpers to keep me warm during my childhood.
- I am happy and grateful that we played board games as children as it filled the evenings during the national power outages.

Exercise 53   Hobbies

I invite you now to complete at least one personal statement in this area that resonates with you. You can utilize part or all of any of the statements above or use something more personal to yourself.

*I am happy and grateful that*_____
_____

4. Contribution

I'm a firm believer that there is always someone in a worse situation than you and that by providing them some assistance it can put your own issues into perspective.

I am not suggesting that you should pity others but merely that by giving in some shape or form you can reinforce your gratitude for what you have.

My first Christmas alone after separating from my wife I volunteered to serve Christmas dinner at the City Mission. I was alone and although I wasn't initially feeling very festive the ability to help others less fortunate than myself reinforced how much I had to be grateful for.

We can all contribute in our own way and I'm certain that for every bit we give we receive ten times as much. This doesn't mean that if you give ten dollars to charity you will receive one hundred dollars back, but more that by giving of ourselves we are opening ourselves up to receiving life's benefits in some way.

> *"We make a living by what we get. We make a life by what we give"* – **Winston S Churchill**

a) Acts of Service

If you have never had a friend who needed a couch to sleep on or a spare bed for the night there is a chance that you will at some stage in your life. What comes around tends to go around so you may find that if you are giving now you may be on the receiving end of that act of kindness at some later date.

> *"No one is useless in this world who lightens the burdens of others"* – **Charles Dickens**

This section of the chapter is for the service you can provide to other beings on this planet and the gratitude that you can allow yourself for being so fortunate.

HOW TO EXERCISE YOUR GRATITUDE MUSCLES

Below is a list of the statements that I use to reaffirm what I have to be grateful for in this area:

- I am happy and grateful that I get to feed the birds and keep their beauty alive through the winter as this contributes to everyone's positive energy.
- I am happy and grateful that I am able to commit some time to soup kitchens as it reminds me how fortunate I am.
- I am happy and grateful that I am able serve Christmas dinner to others less fortunate than me.
- I am happy and grateful that I am able to help others succeed as helping others provides me positive feedback that converts into helping me.
- I am happy and grateful that I have published two non-fiction help books as this allows me to help others succeed.
- I am happy and grateful that I have a spare bedroom that I could provide for a friend at short notice as he had nowhere to stay and I know that he would do the same for me.

Exercise 54   Acts of Service

I invite you now to complete at least one personal statement in this area that resonates with you. You can utilize part or all of any of the statements above or use something more personal to yourself.

*I am happy and grateful that*_____

_____

b) Physical Giving

GRATITUDE FOR HAPPINESS

I'm assuming that you have an excess of something in your life. Whether it's too many clothes, too many books or some other class of belongings, most people in modern society tend to have more of something than they need.

I love the concept of a minimalist wardrobe where you choose one outfit, such as black jeans and a black jumper (a similar wardrobe was utilized by the Apple founder Steve jobs), but like most people I tend to hang on to things I may never wear.

I do have regular clothes culls and have a rule that if a new item of clothing is purchased, I have to dispose of an item it is replacing. To be honest, if you filled my cupboard with cargo pants and V neck T-shirts I could be part Steve Jobs.

Whether you choose to give away all of your property or just buy a cup of coffee for a homeless person, ensure that you avail yourself of the feelings of gratitude that are available to you. To be able to lighten the burden of another is a wonderful thing.

Below is a list of the statements that I use to reaffirm what I have to be grateful for in this area:

- I am happy and grateful that I have surplus clothes that I can give to others to benefit them.
- I am happy and grateful that I have surplus household goods as I am always coming across people who are relocating and it allows me to ease the burden of their move.
- I am happy and grateful that I have a large collection of books as I get to lend them out to benefit others and when some of them aren't returned it's not a big deal.
- I am happy and grateful that I know that if I give something away it always comes back in kind as helping others converts into helping me.

HOW TO EXERCISE YOUR GRATITUDE MUSCLES

- I am happy and grateful that I had a set of spare curtains that I was able to give to someone who had none, enhancing their sleep.
- I am happy and grateful that I had a spare pair of boots that I was able to give to someone who had none as I can only wear one pair of boots at a time.
- I am happy and grateful that I had a spare set of bedding that I was able to give to someone who needed them as this helped me declutter and benefitted another person.

Exercise 55   Physical Giving

I invite you now to complete at least one personal statement in this area that resonates with you. You can utilize part or all of any of the statements above or use something more personal to yourself.

*I am happy and grateful that*_____
_____

Chapter Nine   Travel

Nowadays the word travel tends to conjure up visions of being transported across vast distances. Should we go back only a hundred years in the past, the distances that most people travelled were very limited.

I have been extremely fortunate to have travelled quite a bit in my life. Born in the North of England and now located on the other side of the planet in New Zealand, I can appreciate a plane ride across the planet as much as a walk around the block.

> *"A journey is best measured in friends rather than miles"* – **Tim Cahill**

In this chapter I have provided a variety of gratitude statements designed to cater for most levels of travel. You can choose to be grateful for even the shortest distance and I encourage you to dig deep into your past travels to give you maximum opportunities for gratitude.

1. Overcoming Travel Adversity

No matter how much planning goes into a trip or how luxurious the destination, there is no guarantee of everything being perfect.

Like most people I have had the odd hiccup on my travels. If you have ever navigated the road to the amazing Grand Canyon (in Nevada) you will know that it's a bone shaker. When my wife accompanied me into a majestic pyramid in Egypt she suddenly discovered that she was claustrophobic. My first visit to a tropical island resulted in a bad case of food poisoning. I haven't got a great head for heights so the London Eye and the Eiffel tower were both challenges.

I don't mention these hurdles to diminish the benefits of those great experiences but just to show you that even when you are experiencing some of the events that are on top of your goals lists, they may not be plain sailing.

You get to choose whether to focus on the positives or the negatives of any experience.

When I went up the Eiffel Tower in Paris I managed the first level but continuing up to the summit was too much out of my comfort zone. I could have taken this as a negative and just gone back down to the ground level but there is a bar on the first level of the Eiffel Tower. I chose to make lemons into lemonade and my memory of the Eiffel Tower is sitting down with a Jack Daniels & Coke, looking out over the Champs Elysees on a lovely sunny afternoon.

Below is a list of the statements that I use to reaffirm what I have to be grateful for in this area:

- I am happy and grateful that I live near trees and fields and I can walk in them every day.
- I am happy and grateful that I have looked over the Champs Elysees from the bar up the Eiffel Tower as my limitations resulted in a great memory.
- I am happy and grateful that I endured the bone shaker of a road as this allowed me to look over the Grand Canyon.
- I am happy and grateful that I experienced snorkelling in the clear blue waters off Samoa as I managed to recover from my food poisoning before I left a tropical island.

GRATITUDE FOR HAPPINESS

- I am happy and grateful that I have short legs so that I am comfortable on long haul flights even in economy class.
- I am happy and grateful that I can traverse the world by plane in just over a day.
- I am happy and grateful that I am comfortable staying in a bargain accommodation such as a bed and breakfast.
- I am happy and grateful that I realize that most of the negative things I perceive could go wrong whilst travelling do not actually happen, reducing my stress levels.

Exercise 56 — Overcoming Travel Adversity

I invite you now to complete at least one personal statement in this area that resonates with you. You can utilize part or all of any of the statements above or use something more personal to yourself.

*I am happy and grateful that*_____

_____

2. Little Things Making a Difference

Whether we are travelling short distances or the length of the planet, there are things that can help us personally savour the travel more.

I know it is fashionable for many people to use their smartphone as their time piece nowadays but I still like a wrist watch when travelling. I find it particularly helpful when travelling on long haul flights to set my watch to the local time at the destination and at any time I awake from a slumber I can quickly glance at my watch to orientate myself (without disturbing anyone around me).

HOW TO EXERCISE YOUR GRATITUDE MUSCLES

We all have our own particular idiosyncrasies however far we are travelling and I encourage you to express gratitude for yours in this section.

Below is a list of the statements that I use to reaffirm what I have to be grateful for in this area:

- I am happy and grateful that I have a wrist watch that has an easily adjustable display to make traversing different time zones much simpler.
- I am happy and grateful that I always carry a serviceable pen to allow me to complete boarding cards and other documents quickly.
- I am happy and grateful that I always carry my reading glasses to allow me to complete boarding cards and other documents quickly.
- I am happy and grateful that I experienced an ice cold beer in Caesar's Palace during a hot summer night in Las Vegas as this has created a happy memory that resurfaces whenever I am in a hot place with a cold drink.
- I am happy and grateful that there are in-flight entertainment resources in the backs of airplane seats as this makes long haul flights so much more enjoyable.
- I am happy and grateful that I have a travel pillow as it provides comfort in transit disproportional to its small size.

Exercise 57   Little Things Making a Difference

I invite you now to complete at least one personal statement in this area that resonates with you. You can utilize part or all of any of the statements above or use something more personal to yourself.

*I am happy and grateful that*_____

_____

3. Travelling with Empathy for Others

It is too easy to become agitated when you see people queuing too early to board a plane or carrying a huge case as carryon for a plane that you're boarding. We tend to forget that some people may not be as well travelled as ourselves and they may be experiencing stresses and pressure in their lives.

You have no way of knowing if someone is travelling to a funeral or to visit sick relatives (unless of course you ask) so try to cut your fellow travellers some slack.

We must also realize that as well as encountering fellow travellers we may encounter local residents along our journey and they may not be as affluent as ourselves. People have different opinions that can be influenced by their lives and cultures and these should not be discounted.

By empathizing with the people we encounter when travelling we are allowing ourselves to vibrate at a higher level. I encourage you focus on the positives in these travel situations.

"How people treat you is their karma; how you react is yours" –
Wayne Dyer

Below is a list of the statements that I use to reaffirm what I have to be grateful for in this area:

HOW TO EXERCISE YOUR GRATITUDE MUSCLES

- I am happy and grateful that I travelled from New Zealand to Europe with my partner as I could guard her possessions and allow her to relax in the airport.
- I am happy and grateful that I always carry a spare pen to allow me to help others complete their boarding cards and other travel documents quickly as this reduces their stress creating a calmer environment for me.
- I am happy and grateful that when travelling I can experience other people's cultures and understand how they developed their points of view as this allows me to understand and empathize with them.
- I am happy and grateful that when I am travelling I have surplus funds so if I meet someone who is travelling with limited funds I can pay for the odd drink or meal for them.
- I am happy and grateful that whenever I am backpacking around the world, I relate to the locals I meet with empathy and openness and this allows me to build relationships that benefit us both.
- I am happy and grateful that I have travelled considerably and can provide advice to help enhance the journeys of others.

Exercise 58   Travelling with Empathy for Others

I invite you now to complete at least one personal statement in this area that resonates with you. You can utilize part or all of any of the statements above or use something more personal to yourself.

*I am happy and grateful that*_____

_____

4. Shorter Journeys

When we refer to travel, most people visualize long distances and holidays but having access and appreciating the facilities on our doorstep can provide great inspiration. In New Zealand I notice that around National holidays the majority of people head out of town to camp or play in the great outdoors. I am extremely lucky that I live semi-rural, so rather than having to endure heavy traffic jams and packed campsites I can stay at home and I actually have people wanting to visit me.

If you have ever pitched a tent in your garden as a child you will remember how much fun you can have close to home. Take notice of the resources that are available on your own doorstep or close at hand.

Below is a list of the statements that I use to reaffirm what I have to be grateful for in this area:

- I am happy and grateful that I live close to the beach as I can visit this resource anytime I feel like it.
- I am happy and grateful that I can see the mountains in the distance from my lounge as it reminds me that I have amazing benefits close at hand.
- I am happy and grateful that I have woodland walks outside of my front door as not all amazing journeys have to be lengthy.
- I am happy and grateful that I can get to either the mountains or the beach in only an hour from my house as this provides me lots of travel options.
- I am happy and grateful that as a child our summer holidays involved day trips from home as this allowed us multiple holidays in one summer vacation.

HOW TO EXERCISE YOUR GRATITUDE MUSCLES

- I am happy and grateful that my commute between home and work passes through some amazing countryside that allows me a mini break every day.

Exercise 59   Shorter Journeys

I invite you now to complete at least one personal statement in this area that resonates with you. You can utilize part or all of any of the statements above or use something more personal to yourself.

*I am happy and grateful that*_____

_____

5. Exotic Experiences

Gratitude should come easily and if you have been fortunate enough to experience an exotic or amazing journey then I implore you to remain grateful for it. Just because you experienced a once in a lifetime trip in the past doesn't mean you have to focus on its passing.

By expressing gratitude for that trip it will help you remember the positive emotions and feelings that the trip gave you and add to your happiness. What you class as something special or exotic may not be classed that way by somebody else, but that's ok as this is your gratitude journey.

Below is a list of the statements that I use to reaffirm what I have to be grateful for in this area:

GRATITUDE FOR HAPPINESS

- I am happy and grateful that I have seen the sun set over the Egyptian pyramids as the view was breath-taking.
- I am happy and grateful that I was able to swim with the endangered Hectors dolphins off the coast of New Zealand as this was a gift from my brother and I got to experience it with my wife, creating happy memories for us all.
- I am happy and grateful that I experienced the northern lights on many occasions whilst living in Canada. This was a free entertainment that created happy memories that I can draw on throughout my life.
- I am happy and grateful that I was able to drive through Zion national park whilst travelling to the Grand Canyon. The amazing rock formations of Zion made me feel like I was actually driving through the Grand Canyon.
- I am happy and grateful that I was able to travel through the fjords of Norway as this amazing experience created a happy memory that I will remember throughout my life.
- I am happy and grateful that I have experienced the majesty of travelling on a gondola in Venice as this was a romantic experience.
- I am happy and grateful that I was able to attend an NFL game in New Orleans as the game was an amazing spectacle of entertainment and definitely a tick off my bucket list.

HOW TO EXERCISE YOUR GRATITUDE MUSCLES

Exercise 60   Exotic Experiences

I invite you now to complete at least one personal statement in this area that resonates with you. You can utilize part or all of any of the statements above or use something more personal to yourself.

*I am happy and grateful that*_____

_____

APPENDIX

HOW TO EXERCISE YOUR GRATITUDE MUSCLES

A.1   Alternative ways to use this book

You can probably remember at least one occasion where you committed to a timetable for a course, programme or diet etc. As it progressed you found that it was increasingly difficult to keep to the schedule.

Although you may have heard it said that "you can always find time for something if it is a priority", I want to recognize that we all have different commitments and priorities.

Stage one of the process at the start of this book advocates taking twenty-one days to build your initial list of gratitude statements and distil that list down to three statements.

I believe that using the whole twenty-one days is beneficial as the more you focus on gratitude the more you will benefit. Should you feel that time is an issue you may want to speed up this process.

I have suggested two alternatives below that will allow you to use this book to achieve your gratitude goals at a faster pace.

First Alternative Stage One   Gratitude by Subject

You may have one particular subject that you are currently experiencing a sense of lack about. In order to ease into the gratitude process, we are going to focus on that one subject here.

- Choose one particular subject from the book and read the relevant chapter.
- Commit to following this process for the next five days.

- For each of these five days, start your morning by writing five statements of the things that you are grateful for in that subject.
- Before retiring for bed each night, read your five statements from that morning.
- At the end of the five days you should have approximately twenty-five statements to choose from. If you have duplicated some don't feel bad as the design of the training is to start exercising your gratitude muscles and not to add to your stress.
- Choose the top three statements from your collection that you resonate most with or that you find most empowering and note those down.

HOW TO EXERCISE YOUR GRATITUDE MUSCLES

Second Alternative Stage One   Bingeing on Gratitude

If you're the kind of person who likes to binge-watch the whole season of a TV show on Netflix this option may be for you.

- Set aside enough time to read the book in its entirety.
- As you read through the book, complete the exercise at the end of each section.
- By completing all of the exercises in the chapters you should now have a list of sixty statements.
- Choose the top three statements from your collection that you resonate most with or that you find most empowering and note those down.

Stage Two

The Stage two for these alternative processes is exactly the same as for stage two of this book's initial twenty-one day process.

- Commit to following this process for the next twenty-one days.
- Ensure that you keep your top three statements close at hand.
- For each of these twenty-one days, read your three statements first thing in the morning and last thing at night (preferably out loud).
- Read your three statements at least once more on each of the twenty-one days, at a time that suits you.

HOW TO EXERCISE YOUR GRATITUDE MUSCLES

A.2   Reducing your list to three statements

After working through the exercises and processes in this book, you will have now compiled a large list of gratitude statements.

Narrowing your list down to just three statements may seem daunting for some people but it doesn't need be.

There are two simple steps to this process:

Step 1 Break your list of statements down into manageable chunks (smaller lists):

- If you have written statements covering more than one subject, you may want to split your main list into separate lists for each subject.

Step 2 Read through the smaller lists and choose your top three statements:

- The top three statements don't have to be set in stone, so if you want to pick different statements from your list later, that's fine.
- You can choose statements referring to past events or current events as long as you choose three.

I realize that some people are system orientated and they may want to go through a complex process of rating the statements or comparing and contrasting them.

The more that you complicate things the more it can create procrastination.

You wouldn't go to the gym for an hour and spend fifty minutes walking around the apparatus and only ten minutes working out.

Let's just pick three statements and get on with it!

HOW TO EXERCISE YOUR GRATITUDE MUSCLES

A.3   Suggestions on documenting your statements

With the advent of modern technology, some individuals may not utilize pen and paper at all so I have tried to offer options to suit most readers; but feel free to utilize any option that you feel comfortable with.

A large number of people tend to see their smartphone as another appendage that they keep with them at all times.

If you prefer to work paperless there are multiple opportunities using smartphones and other devices. Below are just a few:

- Type the notes into whatever app or notes platform you use on your smartphone.
- Type the statements into your computer or tablet and send a screenshot of the statements to your smartphone.
- Record yourself speaking the statements into the memo application on your smartphone.
- Use the notes option on your kindle or kindle app to add your statements to this book (if you have also purchased the digital version).

There may be circumstances such as work restrictions, or just personal preferences that necessitate alternatives to carrying your statements digitally. Below are just a few:

- Hand write your three statements on a card or piece of paper small enough to carry in your wallet or pocket (laminating or using a clear protective cover for this method is recommended)

GRATITUDE FOR HAPPINESS

- Type your three statements and print on a card or piece of paper small enough to carry in your wallet or pocket (laminating or using a clear protective cover for this method is recommended)
- Type your three statements and print them at a suitable size to fit into a picture or diploma frame. This is ideal for your office desk etc. to keep them visible while you work.
- If you carry a physical journal (or notebook) write your three statements inside the back cover of the journal.
- Write your statements in the spaces provided within this book (if you have the print version).

I have personally chosen several sets of three statements and have printed them on laminated cards (see the example below). It might seem a bit old school but the beauty of printed cards is that they are accessible all the time. They are not an issue with airport security and can even be read when a plane is taking off or landing.

> I am happy and grateful that I have a roof over my head to protect me from the elements.
>
> I am happy and grateful that I can hear beautiful music as it feeds my spirit.
>
> I am happy and grateful that I have the freedom to determine how I earn my living as this freedom adds to my happiness.

HOW TO EXERCISE YOUR GRATITUDE MUSCLES

If you wish to complete your statements in this book, I have provided the sample beginning "I am happy and grateful that" for the statements at the end of each section.

I have also provided space and the sample beginnings at the end of this book to allow for one hundred and fifty statements.

NB. However you start to use gratitude to help you become happier and more successful, I hope that you start now and continue to use gratitude for the rest of your life. The more you practice gratitude the easier it becomes.

GRATITUDE FOR HAPPINESS

A.4   Your consolidated statements

If you are anything like me, you like to keep all of your reference material together.

I have included this appendix so that you can consolidate your gratitude statements from all of the exercises in the previous chapters.

Feel free to use this area to add extra gratitude statements to the ones you have previously completed. You can never have too many.

I'm assuming that you have been writing statements continually throughout this book, but if you haven't, now is the time to take action!

"To know and not to do is not yet to know" – **Confucius**

1. *I am happy and grateful that* _____
   _____

2. *I am happy and grateful that* _____
   _____

3. *I am happy and grateful that* _____
   _____

HOW TO EXERCISE YOUR GRATITUDE MUSCLES

4. *I am happy and grateful that* _____
   _____

5. *I am happy and grateful that* _____
   _____

6. *I am happy and grateful that* _____
   _____

7. *I am happy and grateful that* _____
   _____

8. *I am happy and grateful that* _____
   _____

9. *I am happy and grateful that* _____
   _____

10. *I am happy and grateful that* _____
    _____

11. *I am happy and grateful that* _____
    _____

GRATITUDE FOR HAPPINESS

12. *I am happy and grateful that* _____
_____

13. *I am happy and grateful that* _____
_____

14. *I am happy and grateful that* _____
_____

15. *I am happy and grateful that* _____
_____

16. *I am happy and grateful that* _____
_____

17. *I am happy and grateful that* _____
_____

18. *I am happy and grateful that* _____
_____

19. *I am happy and grateful that* _____
_____

HOW TO EXERCISE YOUR GRATITUDE MUSCLES

20. *I am happy and grateful that* _____
_____

21. *I am happy and grateful that* _____
_____

22. *I am happy and grateful that* _____
_____

23. *I am happy and grateful that* _____
_____

24. *I am happy and grateful that* _____
_____

25. *I am happy and grateful that* _____
_____

26. *I am happy and grateful that* _____
_____

27. *I am happy and grateful that* _____
_____

GRATITUDE FOR HAPPINESS

28. *I am happy and grateful that* _____
_____

29. *I am happy and grateful that* _____
_____

30. *I am happy and grateful that* _____
_____

31. *I am happy and grateful that* _____
_____

32. *I am happy and grateful that* _____
_____

33. *I am happy and grateful that* _____
_____

34. *I am happy and grateful that* _____
_____

35. *I am happy and grateful that* _____
_____

HOW TO EXERCISE YOUR GRATITUDE MUSCLES

36. *I am happy and grateful that* _____
_____

37. *I am happy and grateful that* _____
_____

38. *I am happy and grateful that* _____
_____

39. *I am happy and grateful that* _____
_____

40. *I am happy and grateful that* _____
_____

41. *I am happy and grateful that* _____
_____

42. *I am happy and grateful that* _____
_____

43. *I am happy and grateful that* _____
_____

GRATITUDE FOR HAPPINESS

44. *I am happy and grateful that* _____
_____

45. *I am happy and grateful that* _____
_____

46. *I am happy and grateful that* _____
_____

47. *I am happy and grateful that* _____
_____

48. *I am happy and grateful that* _____
_____

49. *I am happy and grateful that* _____
_____

50. *I am happy and grateful that* _____
_____

51. *I am happy and grateful that* _____
_____

HOW TO EXERCISE YOUR GRATITUDE MUSCLES

52. *I am happy and grateful that* _____
_____

53. *I am happy and grateful that* _____
_____

54. *I am happy and grateful that* _____
_____

55. *I am happy and grateful that* _____
_____

56. *I am happy and grateful that* _____
_____

57. *I am happy and grateful that* _____
_____

58. *I am happy and grateful that* _____
_____

59. *I am happy and grateful that* _____
_____

GRATITUDE FOR HAPPINESS

60. *I am happy and grateful that* _____
_____

61. *I am happy and grateful that* _____
_____

62. *I am happy and grateful that* _____
_____

63. *I am happy and grateful that* _____
_____

64. *I am happy and grateful that* _____
_____

65. *I am happy and grateful that* _____
_____

66. *I am happy and grateful that* _____
_____

67. *I am happy and grateful that* _____
_____

HOW TO EXERCISE YOUR GRATITUDE MUSCLES

68. *I am happy and grateful that* _____
_____

69. *I am happy and grateful that* _____
_____

70. *I am happy and grateful that* _____
_____

71. *I am happy and grateful that* _____
_____

72. *I am happy and grateful that* _____
_____

73. *I am happy and grateful that* _____
_____

74. *I am happy and grateful that* _____
_____

75. *I am happy and grateful that* _____
_____

GRATITUDE FOR HAPPINESS

76. *I am happy and grateful that* _____
_____

77. *I am happy and grateful that* _____
_____

78. *I am happy and grateful that* _____
_____

79. *I am happy and grateful that* _____
_____

80. *I am happy and grateful that* _____
_____

81. *I am happy and grateful that* _____
_____

82. *I am happy and grateful that* _____
_____

83. *I am happy and grateful that* _____
_____

HOW TO EXERCISE YOUR GRATITUDE MUSCLES

84. *I am happy and grateful that* _____
_____

85. *I am happy and grateful that* _____
_____

86. *I am happy and grateful that* _____
_____

87. *I am happy and grateful that* _____
_____

88. *I am happy and grateful that* _____
_____

89. *I am happy and grateful that* _____
_____

90. *I am happy and grateful that* _____
_____

91. *I am happy and grateful that* _____
_____

GRATITUDE FOR HAPPINESS

92. *I am happy and grateful that* _____
_____

93. *I am happy and grateful that* _____
_____

94. *I am happy and grateful that* _____
_____

95. *I am happy and grateful that* _____
_____

96. *I am happy and grateful that* _____
_____

97. *I am happy and grateful that* _____
_____

98. *I am happy and grateful that* _____
_____

99. *I am happy and grateful that* _____
_____

HOW TO EXERCISE YOUR GRATITUDE MUSCLES

100. *I am happy and grateful that* _____
_____

101. *I am happy and grateful that* _____
_____

102. *I am happy and grateful that* _____
_____

103. *I am happy and grateful that* _____
_____

104. *I am happy and grateful that* _____
_____

105. *I am happy and grateful that* _____
_____

106. *I am happy and grateful that* _____
_____

107. *I am happy and grateful that* _____
_____

GRATITUDE FOR HAPPINESS

108. *I am happy and grateful that* _____
_____

109. *I am happy and grateful that* _____
_____

110. *I am happy and grateful that* _____
_____

111. *I am happy and grateful that* _____
_____

112. *I am happy and grateful that* _____
_____

113. *I am happy and grateful that* _____
_____

114. *I am happy and grateful that* _____
_____

115. *I am happy and grateful that* _____
_____

HOW TO EXERCISE YOUR GRATITUDE MUSCLES

116. *I am happy and grateful that* _____
_____

117. *I am happy and grateful that* _____
_____

118. *I am happy and grateful that* _____
_____

119. *I am happy and grateful that* _____
_____

120. *I am happy and grateful that* _____
_____

121. *I am happy and grateful that* _____
_____

122. *I am happy and grateful that* _____
_____

123. *I am happy and grateful that* _____
_____

GRATITUDE FOR HAPPINESS

124. *I am happy and grateful that* _____
_____

125. *I am happy and grateful that* _____
_____

126. *I am happy and grateful that* _____
_____

127. *I am happy and grateful that* _____
_____

128. *I am happy and grateful that* _____
_____

129. *I am happy and grateful that* _____
_____

130. *I am happy and grateful that* _____
_____

131. *I am happy and grateful that* _____
_____

HOW TO EXERCISE YOUR GRATITUDE MUSCLES

132. *I am happy and grateful that* _____
_____

133. *I am happy and grateful that* _____
_____

134. *I am happy and grateful that* _____
_____

135. *I am happy and grateful that* _____
_____

136. *I am happy and grateful that* _____
_____

137. *I am happy and grateful that* _____
_____

138. *I am happy and grateful that* _____
_____

139. *I am happy and grateful that* _____
_____

GRATITUDE FOR HAPPINESS

140. *I am happy and grateful that* _____
_____

141. *I am happy and grateful that* _____
_____

142. *I am happy and grateful that* _____
_____

143. *I am happy and grateful that* _____
_____

144. *I am happy and grateful that* _____
_____

145. *I am happy and grateful that* _____
_____

146. *I am happy and grateful that* _____
_____

147. *I am happy and grateful that* _____
_____

HOW TO EXERCISE YOUR GRATITUDE MUSCLES

148.   *I am happy and grateful that* _____
_____

149.   *I am happy and grateful that* _____
_____

150.   *I am happy and grateful that* _____
_____

A.5 Glossary

2

20/20 VISION   Classing someone's vision as 20/20 has become commonly known as standard eyesight. The actual numbers in this classification refer to the distance in feet from the chart and the distance at which a normal person can read the same line. If we are 20 feet from the chart and the distance at which a normal person can read the chart is 20 feet we class this as 20/20.

3

3D GLASSES   The 3D in the title is short for 3 Dimensional. When you view a 3D movie at the cinema, the same scene is being projected simultaneously from two different angles. The 3D glasses are designed to line up the pictures so they give the appearance of depth. People who have imperfect eye sight cannot always use 3D glasses as their eyes are unable to focus the two pictures.

9

9/11   September 11th 2001 is known as 9/11 as it is was the eleventh day of the ninth month. It is a famous date because of the terrorist attack on the twin towers of New York's World Trade Centre. Two commercial planes were flown into the towers that day causing their collapse and the death of almost three thousand people.

A

AMYOTROPHIC LATERAL SCLEROSIS (ALS)   One of a group of motor neuron diseases that mainly involve the nerve cells (neurons) responsible for controlling voluntary muscle movement. Over time the symptoms get progressively worse and the death or degeneration of the neurons results in the loss of control of voluntary movement (paralysis).

B

BODY MASS INDEX (B.M.I.)   A scale that is designed to estimate if you are at a healthy weight in relation to your height. Calculated by dividing your weight in kilogrammes by your height (squared) in metres. Example: If you are 80kg in weight and 1.68m tall your B.M.I. = 80 / (1.68x1.68) = 28.35.

C

COHABITATION   The state of living together in an intimate sexual relationship without being married.

COLONEL SANDERS   An American businessman best known for founding the fast food chicken restaurant Kentucky Fried Chicken. Sanders is seen as an inspiration for older people as (after failing 1009 times) he became successful when he was 65.

CONFUCIUS   An influential Chinese philosopher, teacher and political figure born in 551 B.C. His quotes and sayings are still popular today.

D

DISC PROFILING   A personality test designed to identify people's behavioural differences in various situations. Students who take the test are divided into four categories Dominance, Influence, Steadiness and Compliance (DISC).

DRIPPING FLAT CAKE   A large flat bread bun (the width of a dinner plate and approximately two inches deep) smothered in pork dripping (fat). Traditionally found in the north east of England where the fat is usually coated in salt.

E

ECHINACEA   One of a group of flowering plants in the daisy family. Use of this plant extract is purported to promote health by boosting the immune system.

F

FACEBOOK	A social networking website that makes it easy to connect and share with family and friends online.

FOUR EYES	Historically this was a derogatory term for someone who wore spectacles. Typically heard between children in the school yards of England.

FLAT CAKE	A large flat bread bun the width of a dinner plate and approximately two inches deep. Traditionally found in the north east of England

G

GAME OF THRONES	A fantasy television series produced by America's HBO TV Network. The show has various dynasties living in different climates. One of the climates is in a frozen northern area where individuals known as "Watchers" guard a border protected by a huge wall made of ice.

GLASS HALF FULL OR GLASS HALF EMPTY	The term "glass half full" refers to an optimistic perception and the term "glass half empty" refers to a pessimistic view of events. These terms illustrate that in a situation where both statements are actually factual i.e. the glass contains fifty percent of the liquid it can hold, only our frame of mind determines how we perceive the situation.

H

HOME BOX OFFICE (H.B.O.) An American premium cable and satellite television network that is owned by Time Warner.

HELEN KELLER An American author, political activist and lecturer who lived from 1880 to 1968. The first deaf-blind person to earn a Bachelor of Arts degree. Her life story is depicted through the play and film "The Miracle Worker".

K

KEEPING UP WITH THE JONESES There a various stories of how the term originated but it is now an idiom in the modern English language that refers to a situation where one person or more judges their social standing in relation to that of their peers.

KERNEL The edible part of a nut or seed. When talking about a kernel in relation to an idea or education it means something small from which something larger can grow.

L

LOVE LANGUAGES From a book by Dr Gary Chapman that proposes that we can divide the way people express love into five groups (Love Languages). The love languages are Affirmation, Quality Time, Receiving Gifts, Acts of Service and Physical Touch. The theory is that people tend to give love in the way that they prefer to receive love. This can mean that if two people have different love languages, they may be expressing love in abundance but the other partner isn't receiving that love at the same level.

M

MANDY HARVEY A deaf American jazz singer and songwriter who lost her hearing in 2006. She is known for her appearance on the TV show "America's Got Talent" in 2017.

MASLOW'S HIEARACHY OF NEEDS A theory proposed by psychologist Abraham Maslow in 1943. The theory states that there are five interdependent levels of basic human needs that must be satisfied in a strict sequence starting with the lowest level. The five levels are Physiological, Safety, Social, Esteem and finally Self-Actualization.

MORRIS E GOODMAN An American motivational speaker and author. Goodman is also known as "The Miracle Man" as he used his will power to recover from a light plane crash which had left him paralyzed and unable to move, breathe, talk and swallow.

N

NICK VUJICIC An Australian Christian evangelist and motivational speaker born with a rare disorder characterised by the absence of arms and legs. Renowned for the way he has overcome his disability and become an international inspiration.

O

OPERATIONAL TOUR (Tour of duty) A military deployment to a war zone or area of military conflict (traditionally for a set number of months). Members of the various military around the world deploy for various reasons, whether it be humanitarian such as aid distribution or for public relations motives. An operational tour differs from other deployments in that there is a high probability of combat during this period and the troops on that deployment are usually replaced at the end of their tour.

R

ROBERT KIYOSAKI An American self-help, personal finance entrepreneur, guru and author known for his "Rich Dad Poor Dad" series of financial help books.

S

SCUBA DIVING   A method of underwater diving where the diver uses Self-Contained Underwater Breathing Apparatus (SCUBA). This breathing system allows the diver to breathe underwater independently of the surface or any other vessel.

SNORKELLING   Swimming through a body of water wearing a diving mask, a snorkel and sometimes swim fins. The snorkel (breathing tube) allows the swimmer to swim below the surface of the water whilst breathing the air above the surface of the water.

STEPHEN HAWKING   A world renowned theoretical physicist paralysed by Amyotrophic Lateral Sclerosis (ALS) for decades.

T

THOMAS EDISON   An American inventor and businessman. Credited with inventing many of the devices and technologies we take for granted today. Notable inventions are the photograph and the electric light bulb.

W

WETBACK BOILER A system that has an arrangement of water pipes running through the back of a fire. This technique uses the heat from the fire to supplement the heating of the water in a boiler.

Y

YOUTUBE (Youtube.com) A video sharing platform where you can make available a video you have created or view a video others have created. This platform has videos of everything from kittens playing a piano to instructions for you to build a cabin out of logs.

A.6   About the author

I like to think that I have had a very fortunate life, not because I have had a privileged upbringing or have amassed great wealth but because I have focused on the positive aspects in whatever situations I have experienced.

I completed twenty-two years in the British army, over a third of which were spent serving on operational tours such as Iraq or stationed in Northern Ireland during the so-called "troubles". I had a childhood growing up with an outside toilet in the cold winters of Northern England and I have had more than one failed relationship in my adult life. As a "glass half full" type of guy I have chosen to focus on the positives in my life.

I don't presume to compare my past or current circumstances with anyone else and I admit that personally there have been less than ideal situations that have challenged me to see the positive side.

We all have things that we can be grateful about but it can be hard to focus on the positives when we are in a negative state of mind.

I have been as frank as possible when sharing examples from my own life. I hope this has shown you, that we all have areas of our life that could be better.

It is my sincere hope that the information and sample statements in this book help you to realize that you have many areas of your life that you can acknowledge gratitude in.

A Tribute to You, the Reader
I hope that you have enjoyed reading this book as much as I've enjoyed writing it.

It's been a privilege to spend each day reaffirming the things that I am grateful for in my own life and I want you to benefit from this activity too.

I'm sure, having worked through the chapters, that you now have a selection of your own gratitude statements.

When I wrote my annual goals this year I included "To help others succeed" as one of my top goals.

If you have enjoyed this book please feel free to provide feedback with a review on Amazon so that I can reach more people and help more people succeed.

Thank you again for reading this book and investing the time in yourself. I hope that you will continue to build your gratitude muscles.

Below is a statement that everyone reading this book can say out loud and feel proud to do so:-

I AM HAPPY AND GRATEFUL THAT I HAVE CHOSEN TO FOCUS ON THE POSITIVE ASPECTS OF MY LIFE.

www.ingramcontent.com/pod-product-compliance
Lightning Source LLC
Chambersburg PA
CBHW021407290426
44108CB00010B/426